VISUAL QUICKSTART GUIDE

PDF
WITH ACROBAT 4

Ted Alspach

 **Peachpit Press**

Visual QuickStart Guide
PDF with Acrobat 4
Ted Alspach

Peachpit Press
1249 Eighth Street
Berkeley, CA 94710
(510) 524-2178
(510) 524-2221 (fax)

Find us on the World Wide Web at: http://www.peachpit.com

Peachpit Press is a division of Addison Wesley Longman

Editor: Nancy Davis
Production Coordinator: Amy Changar
Compositor: Owen Wolfson
Indexer: Steve Rath

ISBN: 0-201-35461-6

0 9 8 7 6 5 4 3 2 1

Printed and bound in the United States of America

♻ Printed on recycled paper

About the Author

Ted Alspach is the author of more than twenty books on desktop publishing and graphics, as well as hundreds of articles on related topics.

Other recent books by Ted Alspach

PhotoDeluxe 2 for Windows and Macintosh: Visual QuickStart Guide

PageMaker Plus 6.5 for Windows: Visual QuickStart Guide

Illustrator 8 Bible

Illustrator Studio Secrets

Photoshop Complete

Acknowledgments

Even though this book has my name plastered all over it, it has really been the work of several different people; I couldn't ever do a project like this alone. Some of the most important of those people are:

Nancy Davis, my tireless editor at Peachpit, who molded this book from the lump of clay I sent her into the exquisite porcelain vase you have in front of you.

Jennifer Alspach, who updated several of the chapters.

Gage and his brand new little sister Dakota, who continue to provide inspiration.

The Acrobat team at Adobe, which has revolutionized the way that documents are distributed around the world.

Amy Changar, for her production finesse and commitment to making the update of this book look so good.

And everyone at Peachpit Press who helped move this book along until it hit paper.

TABLE OF CONTENTS

TABLE OF CONTENTS

INTRODUCTION

If you've never used Acrobat before, you're in for quite a pleasant experience when you learn about some of the amazing things it can do. If you've only used Acrobat to read PDF documents given to you, you'll be amazed at what can be done on the "other side;" that is, the creation and editing of Acrobat documents. If you've used Acrobat version 3.0.1 or older, you'll be astonished by how many new features and capabilities are included in this release. And if you've used Acrobat 4 at all, this book will guide you through its amazingly deep and complex options, so you can make the most out of your PDF pages.

Acrobat 4 formally declares PDF to be the document exchange format for the masses. Even better, Acrobat Reader is free to everyone with a computer running almost any current system software. So it doesn't matter if you have a Macintosh, a Windows 95 system, an OS/2 system, or even a UNIX-based system.

Over the past few years, PDF has become the standard file format for a variety of uses, including archiving, inter-company publishing, and Web documents. The current format that ships with Acrobat 4.0 is PDF 1.3, which supports many more capabilities than PDF 1.2, which shipped with version 3.0 of Acrobat.

Macintosh and Windows Users

Acrobat was designed to be totally cross platform; the creation and editing software is available on both Macintosh and Windows systems. The resulting PDF files can be viewed on either platform using Acrobat Reader, as well as on other systems, including OS/2 and UNIX.

So, except for a few pages where "Macintosh" or "Windows" is indicated (there are some differences in the print mechanisms of each operating system that are different enough to warrant explanation), each page and example is designed to be used on any platform (currently Macintosh OS 8.x and Windows 98/2000) the Acrobat product family works with.

If you have a UNIX system or a different operating system that Acrobat Reader is created for, the sections on Acrobat Reader will be relevant to you, while the creation and editing sections will not be.

How to Use this Book

If you've never used a Visual QuickStart Guide from Peachpit Press (of which there are dozens, covering every major software package, including ones on PageMaker and PhotoDeluxe by yours truly), then you'll be pleasantly surprised as well. This book works through the basics of Acrobat Reader through the many intricacies of Acrobat itself, in a format that is both easy to understand and fun to read. Examples are presented so you can follow along on your computer, comparing what you see on screen to the pictures on each page. All of the typical tasks you would use Acrobat for are included, as well as other, not-so-common ones that you'll find useful when you start to move beyond the basics.

The book is designed that if you were to read it from front to back, you could do so without having to do any flipping or cross referencing.

Most of the examples are presented in the following fashion:

To work through an example:

1. Find the appropriate topic in the Table of Contents, the Index, or by flipping through the pages looking at the thumb tabs.

2. Go to the page where the example appears. (See, this is easy).

3. Read that example's steps.

4. At your computer, go through the steps one by one, following the directions on each page.

Most of the pages contain just one example with several illustrations and screenshots. The pages before and after each example contain related example tasks that you might find helpful.

Why I'm a PDF Convert

I've been a PDF user ever since Acrobat was first released (version 1.0), but ever since version 3.0 Acrobat has contained the features that I've always wanted. Things like font subset embedding, byte serving capabilities, and compact file sizes (which are almost always much smaller than their original "native" file formats) have made PDF files the standard which no other cross-platform document creator can match.

Some of the exciting new features in version 4.0 include an extremely powerful annotations feature, seamless integration with Photoshop, Illustrator, and InDesign, and even the ability to capture Web pages into PDF documents.

ADOBE ACROBAT BASICS

Adobe Acrobat is truly amazing software. It lets anyone with almost any computer system read any document. It doesn't matter if the document was created with Microsoft Word, QuarkXPress, Adobe InDesign, Adobe Illustrator, or even something as obscure as Jimmy T's Gold Spreadsheet Generator (version 6.0). If you can print some or all of the document from the creating program, that document can be quickly saved as an Acrobat file, commonly known as a Portable Document Format, or PDF.

Anyone with the Acrobat Reader software (which is free) can then open and view the document, with the contents looking exactly the way they did in the original "authoring" program.

The following pages contain an overview of the Acrobat software and the Acrobat process. It's a great way to grasp what Acrobat can do for you.

A Brief History of the World (before Acrobat)

Once upon a time, there was a giant computer in a building on the university of a great campus. Okay, truth be told, the building was the computer. The computer ran on giant vacuum tubes and did such complex computations as figuring out the square root of 16 (which, it turns out, happened to be 4, according to the computing monstrosity). As the first computer ever, there were few compatibility problems with competing software from rival software publishers. Everything was hunky-dory for about thirty years.

At the end of the 1970s, the personal computer revolution began in earnest when two guys in a garage formed Apple Computer. Not long afterwards, other computer manufacturers hopped on the PC (short for Personal Computer back then—you can tell from photos of the 70s that no one cared about that other PC acronym) bandwagon. Suddenly there were all sorts of PCs being made, and there was proprietary software for each computer system.

By the 90s, there were two survivors of the great PC wars, Microsoft and Apple, with various UNIX computer system manufacturers taking up the remaining market share. But a problem remained. How could Joe, who used a PC and Adobe PageMaker, send all his files to his good buddies who used FrameMaker on a UNIX system and QuarkXPress on a Macintosh?

More often than not, Joe would end up printing out his PageMaker documents and his good buddies (who at this time were beginning to distinctly dislike Joe) would have to recreate the documents on their machines, with their software. It was all very frustrating and irritating to Joe and his former friends.

Acrobat to the rescue

When Acrobat 1.0 appeared several years ago, Adobe thought they were solving that very problem; Acrobat users could create Acrobat (PDF) files out of any document, and then that document could be ported to any system, regardless of its hardware or software. The only thing they needed in common was the Acrobat software.

An alternate history of the world (mostly before Acrobat)

The World Wide Web has been around since the 70s. Until just a few years ago, however, no one thought about doing all the cool Web stuff you now see. In a two-year span that the media erroneously refers to as "overnight," the Web became the center of the computer world, overshadowing king-to-be Multimedia and leaving the grand old ruling party of desktop publishing way back in the dust.

Everyone (all the software publishers, anyway) was pretty much caught off guard by the emergence of the Web, including our good buddies at Adobe. Then one day some bright young engineer looked at Acrobat, looked at his Web browser, back at Acrobat, and so on, until he had an idea (not to mention an impending appointment with a chiropractor). Why not use Acrobat to distribute content on the Web? The engineer got really busy and a few weeks (so the legend goes) later, Acrobat 3.0 was available. Acrobat 3 included the ability to create Web pages that aren't that nasty HTML hooey, but instead consisted of beautiful-looking pages with custom fonts and illustrations.

Acrobat 4 upped the ante yet again, now allowing users to convert entire Web sites into PDF documents, complete with active links.

How is Acrobat 4 Different from its Predecessors?

- ◆ Easier conversion of existing documents to PDF than ever before. New methods include printing directly to PDF from the Print dialog box, dragging documents onto the Distiller icon, and opening up non-PDF documents directly in Acrobat.

- ◆ "Exchange" is now just called Acrobat. This is strange for long-time users, but it makes sense overall.

- ◆ The ability to capture Web pages and turn them into fully-linked PDF documents.

- ◆ Advanced Distiller options, including the ability to save sets of options for use at a later time.

- ◆ Annotations, from graphical and text markup tools to recordings and files, that can be appended to a specific location in a document.

- ◆ Automatic bookmarking of Word and other application documents.

- ◆ Two documents can be compared automatically, highlighting the differences between the two.

The Components of Acrobat

Acrobat consists of several "parts," each of which is discussed throughout this book.

- **Acrobat Reader** is the software that allows you to view PDF documents. Acrobat Reader is free and available from Adobe on their Web site, at www.adobe.com.

The commercial version of Acrobat contains the following parts:

- **Acrobat** is the program used to customize PDF files by editing them and adding PDF-specific features like buttons and the ability to download from the Web one page at a time. Before Acrobat 4.0, this application was called Acrobat Exchange.

- **Acrobat Distiller** changes PostScript files into PDF files quickly and easily.

- **Acrobat PDF Writer** is the print driver that generates PDF files within any application. Instead of sending your document to a printer, you create a PDF file using the PDF Writer driver.

- **Acrobat Capture** is a plug-in within Acrobat that lets desktop scanner users scan in documents and convert them to PDFs on the fly. A more robust version is available as a separate product.

The Acrobat Reader Screen and Toolbar

The Acrobat Reader screen (**Figure 1.1**) is a subset of the Acrobat screen. The toolbar along the top and side of the document window provides quick access to most viewing and navigational commands. The Info bar along the bottom provides onscreen information as well as alternative methods for viewing and navigating throughout any PDF document.

The majority of tools in the Acrobat Reader toolbar (**Figure 1.2**) are used for viewing and navigating through PDF documents. Other tools in the toolbar select text and graphics, initiate the Find command, and activate a Web browser.

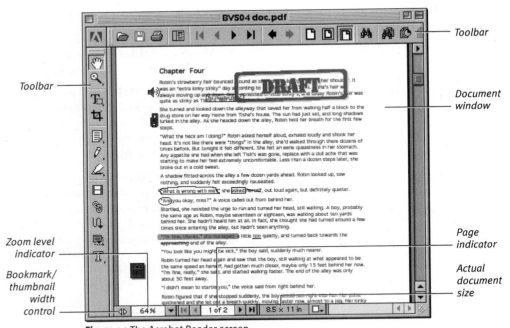

Figure 1.1 The Acrobat Reader screen.

Figure 1.2 The Acrobat Reader toolbar.

Acrobat Mini Glossary

Acrobat (the collection of applications) The collection of software used for creating, editing, and viewing PDF files.

Acrobat (the application) Acrobat is used for viewing and editing PDF files. Acrobat has the ability to add form information, buttons, and other PDF-specific elements to a PDF file. Basic text editing can be done within Acrobat. In this book, I refer to the application as Acrobat, and the files it creates as PDF files.

Adobe Type Manager Software that enables PostScript fonts to be displayed at any point size on screen without a noticeable loss of quality. Adobe Type Manager is often referred to as ATM by Macintosh and Windows users.

Bookmarks Section headings created within Acrobat that provide quick access to specific portions of a PDF document.

Crop To remove excess area around the outside edge of a document page.

Distiller Acrobat Distiller converts PostScript files (including PostScript files printed to disk) into PDF files.

Document A file containing one or more pages of text and/or graphics.

Downsample To lower the resolution (and the file size) of a bitmap image. For instance, a 300 dpi image will often be downsampled to 72 dpi.

FTP File Transfer Protocol. The standard protocol for sending and receiving files on the Internet.

Font Embedding PDF files can include font information within the file, which allows anyone viewing (or printing) the file to view or print the original fonts.

GIF An image format that includes interlacing and transparency, but is typically limited to 256 colors.

HTML HyperText Markup Language. The standard for Web pages on the World Wide Web.

JPEG An image format (JPEG stands for Joint Photographic Experts Group) used to compress images dramatically with a minimum of loss.

Navigation Moving around within a document.

PDF Portable Document Format. The file format used by Acrobat software. PDF files are exactly the same on Windows, Macintosh, and UNIX platforms.

PDF Writer Part of the Acrobat software package, PDF Writer allows any application to print directly to a PDF file.

Plug-ins Additional components added to an application. Acrobat Capture is a plug-in that ships with Acrobat.

PostScript A page-description language developed by Adobe Systems, currently the standard language for laser printers and imagesetters.

Reader Acrobat Reader is used to view and print PDF files.

Search Acrobat Search provides searching capabilities on the text of PDF files.

Thumbnail A miniature version of a document page, shown to the left of the full-size document in Thumbnail view.

Toolbar The rack of tools positioned along the top of the document window.

Acrobat Reader Menus

Figure 1.6 The Tools menu contains commands used for selecting tools and searching for text and notes within PDF documents.

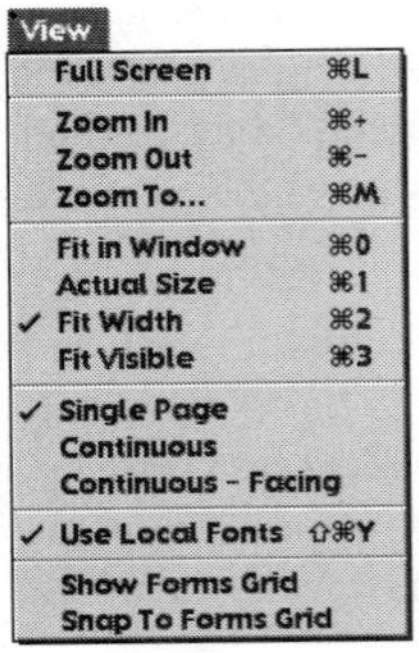

Figure 1.3 The File menu contains commands used for document management.

Figure 1.7 The View menu contains commands used for zooming and other viewing options.

Figure 1.4 The Edit menu contains commands used for retrieving and selecting text and objects with PDF documents.

Figure 1.8 The Window menu contains commands used for displaying and hiding Reader components and PDF document windows.

Figure 1.5 The Document menu contains commands for navigating within PDF documents, as well as commands for changing the structure and contents of a PDF document.

CREATING PDF FILES

PDF files are created by Acrobat software, but most PDF files start out as a different type of document. Some start as ASCII text files. Other, more ambitious documents start as QuarkXPress files and may contain embedded Photoshop and Illustrator files.

This chapter shows you how to use PDF Writer and Acrobat Distiller to create PDF files from the most popular software programs on both Macintosh and Windows platforms.

Using the PDF Writer

PDF Writer allows you to print a file directly to PDF, bypassing the need for Acrobat Distiller.

To use the PDF Writer printer driver to create PDF files on a Macintosh:

1. Select Chooser from the Apple menu.

2. In the Chooser, click on the Acrobat PDFWriter icon (**Figure 2.1**).

3. Click in the upper-left close box to close the Chooser window. Before it closes, you'll see a dialog box reminding you to check Page Setup in your open applications before you print; click the OK button to leave this dialog box.

4. In your application, choose Page Setup from the File menu. Verify that the information there is correct. Click the OK button to verify your changes and close the Page Setup dialog box (**Figure 2.2**).

5. Select Print from the File menu. The dialog box that appears will be different than the standard printer dialog box you're used to. Enter any appropriate information (page range, etc.) and click the OK button.

6. After you click the OK button, a standard file Save dialog box will appear. Enter a name for your PDF file and the location where you'd like to save it, then click the Save button.

✓ Tip

- The PDFWriter icon that appears in the Chooser is an actual file that exists in your Extensions folder. Don't accidentally move or delete this file!

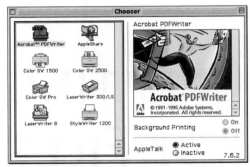

Figure 2.1 Select the Acrobat PDFWriter icon in the Chooser.

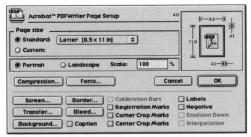

Figure 2.2 Verify all the information is correct in Acrobat PDFWriter Page Setup.

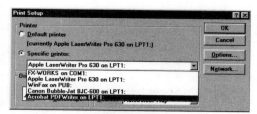

Figure 2.3 Select the Acrobat PDF Writer from the printer list.

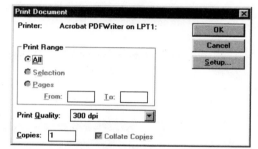

Figure 2.4 Click OK in the Print dialog box to create a PDF file.

To use the PDF Writer printer driver to create PDF files with Windows:

1. Within an application, choose Page Setup from the File menu.

2. In the Print Setup dialog box, select Acrobat PDFWriter from the printer drop-down list (**Figure 2.3**).

3. Click in the upper-right close box to close the Page Setup window.

4. Choose Print from the File menu. The dialog box that appears will be different than the standard printer dialog box you're used to. Enter any appropriate information (page range, etc.) and click the OK button (**Figure 2.4**).

5. After you click the OK button, a standard file Save dialog box will appear. Enter a name for your PDF file and the location where you'd like to save it then click the Save button.

6. After you name the file, you'll be presented with a window for entering PDF Writer information. Entering information is optional. Click OK when you've finished.

USING THE PDF WRITER

Creating PostScript Files

A PostScript file is a file described by the PostScript language. The PostScript language is a computer-to-printer language that is used to describe pages of text and graphics.

To create a PostScript file on a Macintosh:

1. Within any application, choose Print from the File menu.

2. Select the File option in the Destination area of the Print dialog box and click the OK button (**Figure 2.5**).

3. Name the PostScript file and select a location for it.

To create a PostScript file with Windows:

1. Within any application, choose Print from the File menu. The Print dialog box appears.

2. Click the Setup button in the Print dialog box.

3. Click the Properties button in the Page Setup dialog box. The Properties window for that printer will be displayed.

4. Click the PostScript tab (**Figure 2.6**).

5. Choose the Encapsulated PostScript (EPS) option from the pop-up menu. Click OK.

6. Click OK to exit the Page Setup dialog box. Click OK in the Print dialog box, and the PostScript file will be created.

✓ Tip

■ PDF files can be created from existing PostScript files (see above for more on how to create PostScript files).

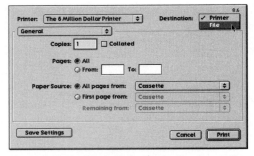

Figure 2.5 Select File from the Destination pop-up list in the Print dialog box.

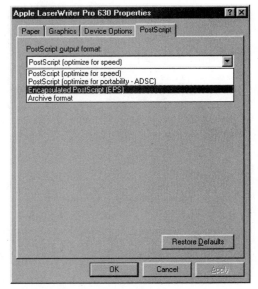

Figure 2.6 Select the EPS option in the PostScript tab of the Printer Properties dialog box.

To create a PDF file with Acrobat Distiller (Mac and Windows):

1. Select the PostScript file that you want to convert into a PDF file.

2. Drag the PostScript file on top of the Acrobat Distiller icon.

3. Acrobat Distiller will automatically "distill" the PostScript file into a PDF file, adding the ".PDF" tag to the end of the file name. For example, a PostScript file called "QuickStart.ps" would be saved by Distiller as "QuickStart.ps.pdf."

✓ Tip

■ Distiller options are discussed in detail in Chapter 5, *Using Acrobat Distiller with PostScript Files.*

CREATING POSTSCRIPT FILES

ACROBAT
READER BASICS

Acrobat Reader is software that allows anyone to read PDF (Portable Document Format) files. There's a Reader for Macintosh, Windows, and UNIX platforms, and all PDF files are completely cross-platform. No matter which system the original PDF file was created on, it can be read on any other system. This is just one of the strengths of Acrobat Reader.

To make sure everyone can get Acrobat Reader to read any PDF files, Adobe provides the software free on the official Adobe Web site (www.adobe.com). The software is easy to install (see the next two pages for installation instructions for Macintosh and Windows systems), and it only takes up a few megabytes of hard disk space. Acrobat Reader needs about 4MB of RAM to run.

An additional component of the Reader software allows it to be used within popular Web browsers like Netscape Navigator, enabling it to read one page at a time from Web sites all over the world.

Installing Acrobat Reader for Macintosh

To install Acrobat Reader on your Macintosh:

1. Find the Acrobat Reader Installer icon and double-click on it (**Figure 3.1**). This launches the installation software.

2. Click the Continue button when the main screen appears.

3. Select the folder and disk in which you want to install the software, and then press the Install button. If you don't specify a location, the default location will be the top level of your startup drive (**Figure 3.2**). The installer automatically quits any applications that had been running. As Acrobat Reader installs itself, a progress bar that pops up across your screen fills in from left to right. You can stop the installation at any time by clicking the Stop button.

4. After installation is complete, click the Restart button in the dialog box. Your computer will restart, loading any new system extensions required for Acrobat reader.

5. Verify Acrobat Reader has been installed properly by opening the folder where it was installed (**Figure 3.3**).

✓ Tip

- For best results, restart your Macintosh with extensions off (press the Shift key during startup) when installing new software.

Figure 3.1 Double-click the Reader Installer.

Figure 3.2 Select the disk and folder before clicking the Install button.

Figure 3.3 After restarting your Macintosh, the Acrobat Reader application will be fully installed and ready to use.

Figure 3.4 Double-click on the Reader Installer icon.

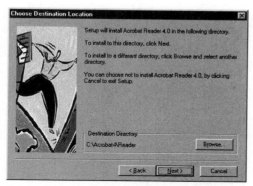

Figure 3.5 Choose the Directory path before clicking the Next button.

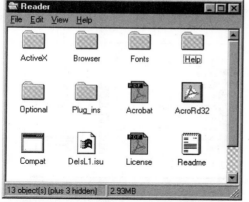

Figure 3.6 The Acrobat Reader Application window shown after installation.

Installing Acrobat Reader for Windows

To install Acrobat Reader on your Windows system:

1. Find the Acrobat Reader Installer file and double-click on it (**Figure 3.4**). This launches the installation software.

2. Click the Next button when the Welcome screen appears.

3. Click the Accept button on the Software License Agreement screen.

4. The installer will select a location on your hard drive automatically, and display the directory path in the Destination Directory window (**Figure 3.5**).

   To change the directory, click the Browse button. If the directory is correct, click the Next button.

   As Acrobat Reader installs itself, a progress bar pops up on your screen and fills in from left to right. You can stop the installation at any time by clicking the Cancel button.

5. After installation, click the Finish button. Click OK in the dialog box that follows. The Installer will then quit.

6. Verify Acrobat Reader has been installed properly by opening the directory where it was installed (**Figure 3.6**).

Using Acrobat Reader

To run Acrobat Reader:

Double-click on the Acrobat Reader icon (located in the Acrobat Reader folder) (**Figure 3.7**).

To open an existing PDF file n Acrobat Reader:

1. Choose Open from the File menu (**Figure 3.8**).

2. Select the file you wish to open and click the Open button (**Figure 3.9**).
    or
    Double-click on the PDF file icon (**Figure 3.10**).
    or
    Drag the PDF file icon on top of the Acrobat Reader icon.

To close an open PDF file:

◆ Choose Close from the File menu.
    or
    (Macintosh) Click the close box in the upper-left corner of the document window.
    or
    (Windows) Click the close (X) box in the upper-right corner of the document window.

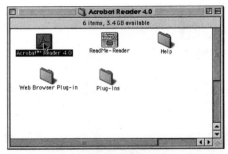

Figure 3.7 Double-click on the Acrobat Reader icon to run the application.

Figure 3.8 From the File menu, choose Open.

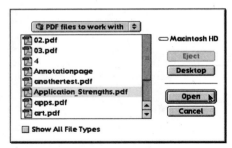

Figure 3.9 Select the file from the file list within the Open dialog box.

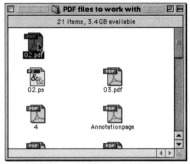

Figure 3.10 Double-click on a PDF file to open it in Acrobat Reader.

Figure 3.11 The Zoom tool is accessible from the toolbar positioned under the menu bar.

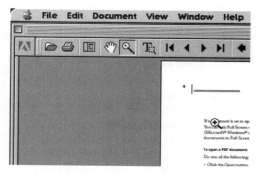

Figure 3.12 Click on the area of a document you wish to zoom in on.

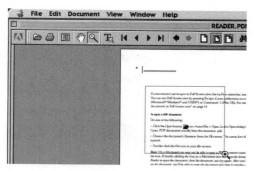

Figure 3.13 To zoom in on a specific area, drag around that area with the Zoom tool.

To zoom in on a PDF document:

1. Select the Zoom tool on the Acrobat tool-bar (**Figure 3.11**).

2. Click on the area you wish to zoom in on (**Figure 3.12**). Releasing the mouse button magnifies that area.

To zoom in on a specific area of a PDF Document:

1. Select the Zoom tool on the Acrobat toolbar.

2. Drag a marquee (a rectangular dashed line) with the Zoom tool around the particular area you want to zoom in on (**Figure 3.13**). That area will fill the screen when you release the mouse button.

✓ Tip

- Each click of the Zoom tool doubles the current magnification (from 100% to 200% to 400% and so on).

USING ACROBAT READER

To zoom out of a PDF document:

1. Select the Zoom tool from the toolbar (**Figure 3.14**).

2. Press the Option key (Mac) or Control key (Windows). The middle of the magnifying glass will display a minus (−) sign (**Figure 3.15**).

3. Click while pressing the Option or Control key (**Figure 3.16**). The page will zoom out to one-half the previous magnification (i.e., 100% will become 50%, 50% will become 25%) (**Figure 3.17**).

✓ Tip

■ To access the Zoom tool using the keyboard, press Z.

Figure 3.14 The Zoom tool is accessible from the toolbar positioned under the menu bar.

Figure 3.15 The Magnifying Glass (Zoom tool) will display a minus sign when the Option key (Mac) or Control key (Windows) is pressed.

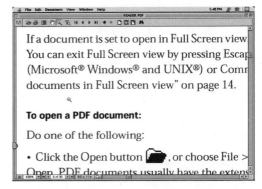

Figure 3.16 Click on the document with the Zoom Out tool.

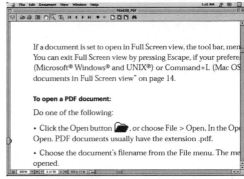

Figure 3.17 The page is reduced to one-half the previous zoom setting.

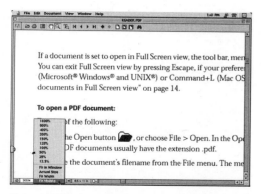

Figure 3.18 The zoom level pop-up menu is found in the lower left of each document window.

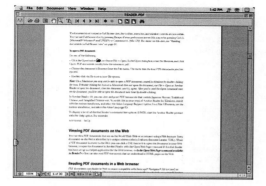

Figure 3.19 Once you select a zoom level from the zoom level pop-up menu, the document will zoom to that size.

Figure 3.20 The View menu provides another method for selecting preset zooms.

In addition to using the Zoom tool to change the magnification of your document, there are several different preset zoom levels that are easily accessible from within Acrobat Reader.

To use the preset zoom levels:

1. Press and hold on the zoom level indicator along the lower left of the document window (**Figure 3.18**).

2. Select a preset zoom from the menu that appears.

3. The document displays at the size you select (**Figure 3.19**).
   or
   Select a preset zoom level from the available options under the View menu (**Figure 3.20**). The View menu only shows the named views (Fit in Window, Actual Size, Fit Width, Fit Visible).

✓ Tip

- Fit in Window, Fit Width, and Fit Visible are arbitrary zoom levels with no particular zoom percentage assigned to them. The resulting zoom percentage is based on the window size of the current document.

USING ACROBAT READER

It's also possible to view your document at a specific zoom level percentage that isn't one of the preset zoom levels.

To display a document at a specific zoom level:

1. Press Command+M (Macintosh) or Control-M (Windows) to access the Zoom To dialog box.
   or
   Select Zoom To from the View menu (**Figure 3.21**). The Zoom To dialog box appears (**Figure 3.22**).

2. Type the magnification you desire and click the OK button or press the Enter key. The document will be displayed at the magnification you specified.

To hide everything but the document:

◆ Choose Full Screen from the View menu (**Figure 3.23**). Everything but the current document will be hidden, including the menu bar and other application windows (**Figure 3.24**).

To "unhide" everything that was hidden:

◆ Press the ESC key on your keyboard. The document will display at the previous view (as it was displayed prior to viewing the document in Full Screen mode).

✓ Tips

■ To quickly enter Full Screen mode, press Command-L (Macintosh) or Control+L (Windows).

■ Working in Full Screen mode requires that you know many of the key commands for navigating and zooming within Acrobat Reader.

Figure 3.21 Select Zoom To from the View menu.

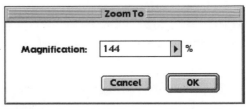

Figure 3.22 Enter your desired magnification in the Zoom To dialog box and click the OK button or press the Enter key.

Figure 3.23 Choose Full Screen from the View menu to hide everything but the document.

Figure 3.24 Full Screen mode hides everything that isn't part of your PDF document.

Figure 3.25 Select the Hand tool to move the document within the document window.

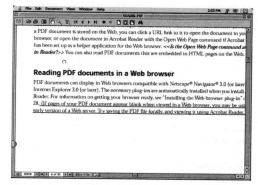

Figure 3.26 Click and drag to reposition a document within the window.

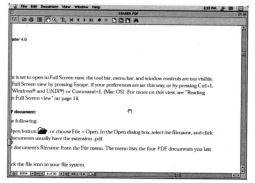

Figure 3.27 Release the mouse button and the page will stay in the new position.

Navigating a PDF Document

Many Acrobat pages are too large to fit on your monitor at a size to be read without incurring permanent squint damage. Unfortunately, this means part of the page is cropped by the edge of your monitor, or more accurately, by the edge of your document window. And, since everyone knows that scroll bars are way too inconvenient to use all the time, Acrobat Reader provides several other methods for navigating within a single document page.

To move around freely within a page:

1. Select the Hand tool from the toolbar along the top of the page (**Figure 3.25**).

2. Click on the page and drag (keep the mouse button pressed as you move the mouse) to reposition the page (**Figure 3.26**).

3. Release the mouse button and the page will stay at the new position (**Figure 3.27**).

To move down within a page:

◆ Press the Down Arrow key on your keyboard.

To move up within a page:

◆ Press the Up Arrow key on your keyboard.

✓ Tip

■ Press the Page Down key when the bottom of a page is showing to move to the top of the next page in the document. Likewise, press the Page Up key when the top of a page is showing to move to the previous page.

To view the next page in a document:

◆ Press the Page Down key.
or
Choose Next Page from the Document menu.

To view the previous page in a document:

◆ Press the Page Up key.
or
Choose Previous Page from the Document menu.

To go to a specific page in a document:

1. Choose Go To Page from the Document menu (**Figure 3.28**).

2. In the Go To Page dialog box, enter the page that you'd like to go to and click the OK button or press Enter (**Figure 3.29**).

To go to the first page in a document:

◆ Choose First Page from the Document menu.
or
Press the Home key.

To go to the last page in a document:

◆ Choose Last Page from the Document menu.
or
Press the End key.

✓ Tip

■ Use the toolbar to quickly navigate within any document.

Figure 3.28 To go to any page within a document choose Go To Page from the Document menu.

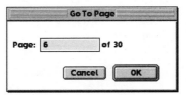

Figure 3.29 Enter a page number in the Go To Page dialog box and click the OK button to go to that page.

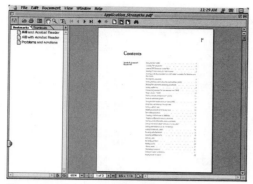

Figure 3.30 Choosing Show Bookmarks from the Window menu shows the Bookmarks on the left side of a page. Use the bookmarks to quickly jump to a specific location within a document.

Figure 3.31 Click on the Show/Hide Navigation button.

Multiple viewing options

You will find viewing options under the View menu.

Full Screen is the view where only the page (and not the toolbars, menu bar, or any other Acrobat element) is showing. This is the default view.

Bookmarks are little markers created within Acrobat that provide a way to get to a specific section of a page instantly.

Thumbnails are small representations of the pages within the document. These are useful for finding a page based on its appearance.

To view the document only:

◆ Choose Full Screen from the View menu.

To view a document with Bookmarks:

◆ Choose Show Bookmarks from the Window menu (**Figure 3.30**).
  or
  Click on the Show/Hide Navigation button on the toolbar.

To view a document with Thumbnails:

◆ Choose Thumbnails from the Document menu.
  or
  Click on the Show/Hide Navigation button (**Figure 3.31**) on the toolbar to view the Navigation palette, then click on the Thumbnails tab.

✓ Tip

■ Bookmark and Thumbnail views reduce the page size substantially on screen, often making text difficult to read.

To use Bookmarks to go to a specific spot within a document:

1. Click the Show/Hide Navigation button on the toolbar.

2. Click the Bookmarks tab (**Figure 3.32**). Click on the Bookmark that describes the spot you want to view. The page and location of that Bookmark will appear on the screen (**Figure 3.33**).

To use Thumbnails to go to a specific page within a document:

1. Click the Show/Hide Navigation button on the toolbar (**Figure 3.34**).

2. Click the Thumbnails tab (**Figure 3.35**). Click on the Thumbnail that represents the page you want to view. That page will appear on the screen.

✓ Tip

■ Bookmarks contain location information (page and position) and zoom level information. They are often used to highlight a small portion of a document, forcing that small portion to fill up the entire viewing area.

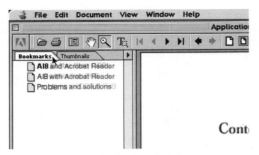

Figure 3.32 Click on the Bookmarks tab.

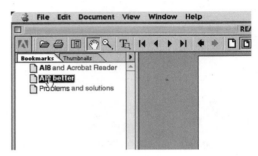

Figure 3.33 Click on the Bookmark you want to see and you'll go there instantly.

Figure 3.34 Click on the Show/Hide Navigation button.

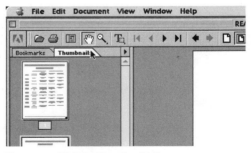

Figure 3.35 Click the Thumbnail tab.

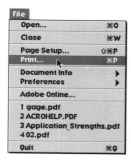

Figure 3.36 Choose Print from the File menu.

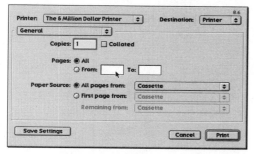

Figure 3.37 In the Print dialog box, enter the number of copies and the page range. Then click the Print button.

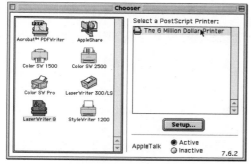

Figure 3.38 The Chooser window allows you to select a printer.

Printing a PDF Document

To print a PDF document from Acrobat Reader (Macintosh):

1. Choose Print from the File menu (or press Command+P) (**Figure 3.36**).

2. Enter the number of copies in the Print dialog box (**Figure 3.37**).

3. Enter the page range (starting and ending page numbers) in the From and To text fields.

4. Click the Print button to send the document to the printer. Clicking Cancel returns you to your document without printing anything.

✓ Tip

- Acrobat Reader (or the full Acrobat product) must have been installed via the Installer in order to print documents correctly.

To choose a printer (Macintosh):

1. Select Chooser from the Apple menu (at the far left of the menu bar).

2. Click on the LaserWriter icon in the Chooser window (**Figure 3.38**). If printing to another type of printer, click on the appropriate printer type.

3. Select the printer from the list of printers (hey, even if you only have one printer, it's still a list).

4. Close the Chooser window. The next time the Print dialog box opens, the new printer will be selected.

PRINTING A PDF DOCUMENT

To print a PDF document from Acrobat Reader (Windows):

1. Choose Print from the File menu (or press Control+P) (**Figure 3.39**).

2. Enter the number of copies in the Print dialog box (**Figure 3.40**).

3. Enter the page range (starting and ending page numbers) in the From and To text fields.

4. Click the OK button to send the document to the printer. Clicking Cancel returns you to your document without printing anything.

To select a printer (Windows):

1. Choose Print Setup from the File menu (or press Control+Shift+P).

2. The Print Setup dialog box appears (**Figure 3.41**).

3. Select the printer from the Name dropdown menu.

4. Change any other options as needed.

5. Click the OK button. The new printer will receive future printouts.

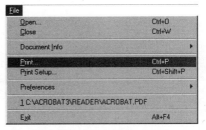

Figure 3.39 Choose Print from the File menu.

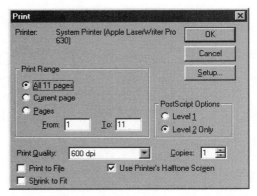

Figure 3.40 In the Print dialog box, enter the number of copies and the page range and then click the OK button.

Figure 3.41 In the Print Setup dialog box, select the printer you wish to print to.

ACROBAT READER IN DEPTH

4

Now that you've mastered the basics of Acrobat Reader, it's time to move on to some of the more advanced features of Reader that make it such wonderful software for viewing documents.

Often you'll want to go beyond simple document navigation and viewing, to do things such as searching your document for text, copying text or an image from Acrobat Reader, or even changing the many preferences that Reader provides.

This chapter takes you on a tour of Acrobat Reader's nitty-gritty details, so you can make the software work for you!

Understanding Your PDF Document

Each PDF document has certain information associated with it. This information may tell you when the document was created, what application created it, or when it was last modified.

To read the Document Info for the current document:

1. Choose General from the Document Info submenu in the File menu. You can also press Command-D (Macintosh) or Control+D (Windows) (**Figure 4.1**). The General Info dialog box appears, showing various information (**Figure 4.2**). Note that there are four uneditable text boxes in this dialog box: Title, Subject, Author, and Keywords. These boxes are editable only within Acrobat.

   The "Optimized" (in this case set to Yes) label refers to the capability of Acrobat 4 to compress PDF files, allowing them to be read one page at a time via Web browsers and the Acrobat Reader Plug-in.

2. To close the General Info dialog box, click the OK button.

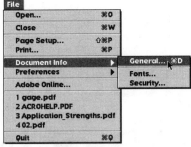

Figure 4.1 Choose General from the Document Info submenu of the File menu.

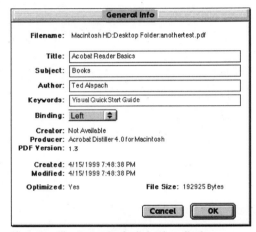

Figure 4.2 The General Info dialog box displays information about the current active document.

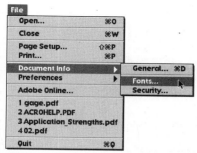

Figure 4.3 Choose Fonts from the Document Info submenu of the File menu.

To determine which fonts are used in a PDF document:

1. Choose Fonts from the Document Info submenu in the File menu (**Figure 4.3**). A list of all the "base" fonts used in the document appears in the Font Info window (**Figure 4.4**).

2. Click the List All Fonts button to see an expanded list of fonts that includes basic styles (bold and italic) applied to fonts within the document (**Figure 4.5**). This listing more accurately depicts the fonts that are used within the PDF file.

3. Click the OK button to close the Font Info window.

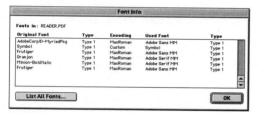

Figure 4.4 The Font Info window displays the base fonts used in the PDF document.

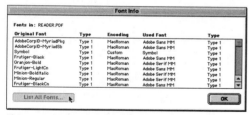

Figure 4.5 Clicking the List All Fonts button shows all variations of fonts used in the PDF file.

Securing Your Document

Various levels of security can be applied to any PDF document. These options can prevent someone viewing a PDF document from changing the document (in Acrobat), printing the document, opening the document, selecting text and graphics, and adding or changing notes and form fields.

Many of these activities can't be done in Reader because it doesn't have the capability to do such things as changing the document and adding or changing notes and form fields. Those items will always read "Not Allowed" when viewed in Reader, but may show up as "Allowed" in Acrobat (which has the tools for doing both of those activities).

To look at the Security options:

1. Choose Security from the Document Info submenu in the File menu (**Figure 4.6**). The Security Info dialog box will appear, displaying all the current security information (**Figure 4.7**).

2. To close the Security Info dialog box, click the OK button.

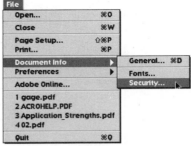

Figure 4.6 Choose Security from the Document Info submenu on the File menu.

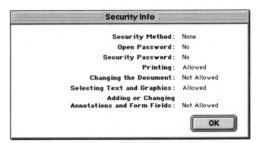

Figure 4.7 The Security Info dialog box displays the security options for the current active document.

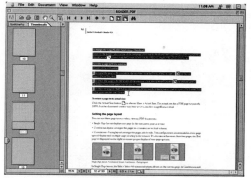

Figure 4.8 Choose the Text Select tool from the toolbar.

Figure 4.9 Drag across the text that you want to select, with the Text Select tool.

Selecting and Working with Text and Graphics

To be able to do anything with text or graphics, you first need to know how to select text or graphics.

To select text:

1. Choose the Text Select tool on your toolbar (**Figure 4.8**).

2. Drag the Text Select tool over the text that you would like to select (**Figure 4.9**). The Text Select tool selects entire words at once. There is no way to select just a portion of a word.

   See the next page for details on how to copy and paste the text you've selected.

Selecting text is pretty straightforward, but selecting graphics is not. In fact, you never actually select graphics. Instead, Acrobat provides a Graphics Select tool that lets you take a screenshot of a portion of your Reader document (which may include graphics). For graphics which normally print well and display poorly, this tool is practically useless.

To select graphics within a PDF document:

1. Choose the Graphics Select tool from the pop-up tools found with the Text Select tool (**Figure 4.10**).

2. Drag the Graphics Select tool over the area that you would like to select (**Figure 4.11**).

   The pixels within the selection border represent the area that is selected.

   See the next section for details on how to copy and paste the pixels you've selected.

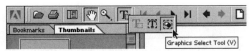

Figure 4.10 The Graphics Select tool is found with the pop-up tools of the Text Select tool.

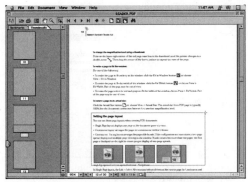

Figure 4.11 With the Graphics Select tool, drag across the area of the page you want to select.

Figure 4.12 Choose Copy from the Edit menu.

Figure 4.13 In another application, choose Paste from the Edit menu.

To cut, copy, and paste selected text or graphics within Acrobat Reader:

Okay, the truth is, you can't cut text or graphics in Acrobat Reader. And you can't paste, either. But you can copy, and you can paste what you've copied into another application. So this should really be:

To copy selected text or graphics within Acrobat Reader:

◆ With either text or graphics selected, choose Copy from the Edit menu (**Figure 4.12**).

The text or graphics will be copied and be available for pasting in another application.

To paste copied text or graphics in other applications:

◆ In any program (other than Acrobat Reader), choose Paste from the Edit menu (**Figure 4.13**).

The copied text or graphics will appear in the active document of the application.

Does not paste into Pagemaker 5.

SELECTING AND WORKING WITH TEXT AND GRAPHICS

Changing Reader Preferences

Usually, the default magnification at which PDF files are displayed is preset to a view that may not be the best for your monitor. Fortunately, you can change this setting within Acrobat Reader's preferences.

To change the default magnification:

1. Choose General from the Preferences submenu in the File menu (**Figure 4.14**). The General Preferences dialog box appears.

2. Select a new default magnification from the Default Zoom pop-up menu, or type in a new percentage in the text field (**Figure 4.15**).

3. Click the OK button (or press Return or Enter).

   The new default magnification is now in place. All documents opened in Reader from this point on will be displayed at the new default magnification.

✔ Tip

■ Many Acrobat Reader users prefer to have one of the "Fit" settings as their default. The Fit Visible option is great for focusing on the content within a page instead of seeing all the white space around that content.

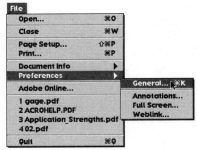

Figure 4.14 Select General from the Preferences submenu in the File menu.

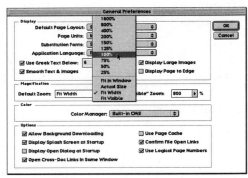

Figure 4.15 Select a new default magnification from the pop-up menu.

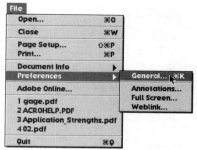

Figure 4.16 Choose General from the Preferences submenu of the File menu.

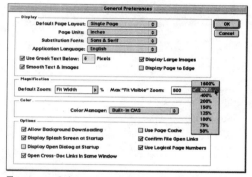

Figure 4.17 Select a new default magnification from the pop-up menu.

If you've ever seen Acrobat zoom in too far when you've changed pages in Fit Visible mode to the point where just one word fills your 37-inch monitor, you'll appreciate Acrobat Reader's ability to restrict Fit Visible's maximum zoom amount. This prevents pages with just a page number on them from scaring you to death with giant numbers.

To modify maximum resolution in the Fit Visible setting:

1. Choose General from the Preferences submenu in the File menu (**Figure 4.16**). The General Preferences dialog box appears.

2. Select a new zoom percentage from the pop-up menu next to Max "Fit Visible" Zoom, or type in a new value in the text field (**Figure 4.17**).

3. Click the OK button. Now, the Fit Visible magnification setting will never exceed the maximum zoom percentage you've entered.

There are a multitude of preferences that can be changed in Acrobat Reader to affect the way you view and navigate through documents. Most of these can be modified through the General Preferences dialog box.

Keep in mind that changes made in Acrobat Reader affect the way you'll view and work with all future documents within Reader only. These changes aren't tied to specific documents, they only affect the way Reader displays documents. To change document preferences you must edit the document in Acrobat.

To change other Reader preferences:

1. Choose General from the Preferences submenu in the File menu (**Figure 4.18**).

2. Make any desired changes in the General Preferences dialog box (**Figure 4.19**).

3. Click the OK button. All changes you've made affect the current and future documents opened in Reader. If you don't like your changes, just re-open the General Preferences dialog box and undo your changes.

✔ Tip

■ If another person uses Acrobat Reader on the machine where you've made your changes, keep in mind that he or she will be stuck with your preferences changes.

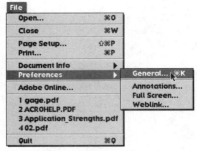

Figure 4.18 Choose General from the Preferences submenu of the File menu.

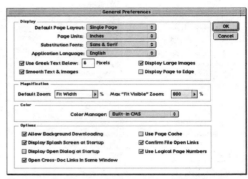

Figure 4.19 Make any changes in the General Preferences dialog box and then click the OK button.

Figure 4.20 Choose Full Screen from the View menu.

Figure 4.21 The Full Screen mode hides the menu bar and toolbar, and zooms the page to fill the screen.

Utilizing the Full Screen Mode

Acrobat Reader 4 has a special "Presentation" mode called Full Screen mode. In this mode, Acrobat Reader documents can display like a slide show, or similar to the way that presentation software like Adobe Persuasion or Microsoft PowerPoint displays screens.

To change to Full Screen mode:

◆ Choose Full Screen from the View Menu (**Figure 4.20**).

The screen will redraw, zooming the current page to the full size of the screen, hiding the menu bar and toolbar (**Figure 4.21**).

To exit Full Screen mode:

◆ Press the ESC key (in the upper left of the keyboard).

The screen will redraw, displaying the menu bar and toolbar, and zooming the current page back to the view that was used prior to the Full Screen mode.

Without a menu bar or toolbar displayed on screen, Acrobat Reader becomes slightly more difficult to use. If you're like most people, you don't have an extra 2Mb of storage space in your brain to memorize all the Acrobat key commands. Fortunately, there are several preferences for Full Screen mode that can make navigating much easier than it would be otherwise.

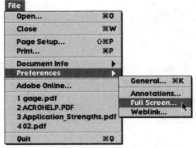

Figure 4.22 Choose Full Screen from the Preferences submenu of the File menu.

To change the Full Screen Preferences:

1. Choose Full Screen from the Preferences submenu in the File menu (**Figure 4.22**).

2. In the Full Screen Preferences dialog box, make any changes that you believe will make it easier to work in Full Screen mode (**Figure 4.23**).

3. Click OK when you've finished making changes to save those changes.

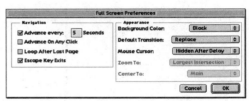

Figure 4.23 Make any desired changes in the Full Screen Preferences dialog box and click OK.

✔ Tip

■ When giving a presentation, the Advance On Any Click option is very useful. Remember you can always use the Left Arrow or Page Up keys to go back a page if the need arises.

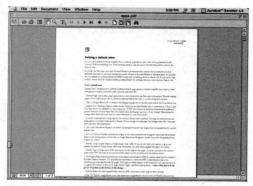

Figure 4.24 Notes appear as little document icons on a PDF document page.

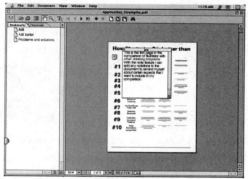

Figure 4.25 Double-clicking on the note icon displays its contents. Clicking the close box on the expanded note collapses it back to an icon.

Reading Notes

When a PDF file is edited in Acrobat , annotations can be added to the document in any area. These notes resemble a tiny document icon when viewed in Acrobat Reader; the text of the note is hidden by default within the little icon (**Figure 4.24**).

To read Acrobat Reader notes:

1. Locate the note that you wish to read on a PDF document.

2. Double-click on the note with the cursor. The note will expand to display all its text (**Figure 4.25**).

To close expanded Acrobat Reader notes:

◆ Click the close box (in the upper-left corner) of the note.

   The note will collapse back to the little document icon.

✔ Tip

■ In Acrobat Reader, you may click on a note once and drag it around a page, but you may not delete or remove that note. In addition, because you can't save changes to a PDF document in Reader, the note will reappear in its original position the next time you open that document in Reader.

Arranging Multiple Windows

Your computer monitor can get quite messy if you have several Acrobat PDF document windows open at one time in Reader. Fortunately, there are some built-in functions that "clean up" your document windows automatically.

To quickly display all open documents:

◆ From the Tile submenu of the Window menu, choose either Horizontally or Vertically (**Figure 4.26**).

Tile Horizontally displays open windows one above another in a vertical stack (**Figure 4.27**).

Tile Vertically displays open windows next to each other in a horizontal stack (**Figure 4.28).**

Figure 4.26 Select a Tile option from the Window menu.

Figure 4.27 Tile Horizontally displays documents one above another.

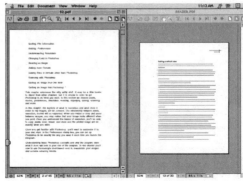

Figure 4.28 Tile Vertically displays documents next to each other.

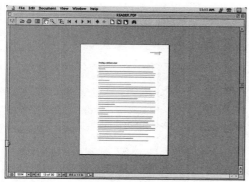

Figure 4.29 Cascade displays the active document in front of the other open documents.

Figure 4.30 Choosing Close All from the Window menu closes all open documents without quitting Acrobat.

Figure 4.31 Choosing Quit from the File menu automatically quits Reader and closes any open documents.

To bring the active window to the front while displaying the title bars of other open documents:

◆ Choose Cascade from the Window menu.

The active (selected) document will appear in the front, while behind it the title bars of all the other documents will be displayed (**Figure 4.29**).

To close all open documents at once without quitting:

◆ Choose Close All from the Window menu (**Figure 4.30**).

Because Acrobat Reader can't save changes to documents, you'll never be presented with a "Do You Wish To Save Changes" dialog box. Instead, the documents will quickly zip away.

or

Option-click for Macintosh or Alt-click for Windows on the close box of any open documents. This closes all open documents instantly.

To close all open documents at once when quitting Acrobat Reader:

◆ Choose Quit from the File menu. Any open documents automatically close when the program is quit (**Figure 4.31**).

ARRANGING MULTIPLE WINDOWS

Using the Find Tool

Sometimes it is necessary to locate a particular phrase or word within a document. Instead of searching through the document by reading every page, you can use Acrobat Reader's Find command to do the work for you.

To find a word in a PDF document:

1. Choose Find from the Edit menu (**Figure 4.32**). The Find dialog box appears.

2. Type the word (or words) that you're looking for in the text field (**Figure 4.33**). If the word stands alone (like PDF), then check the Match Whole Word Only checkbox.

3. Click the Find button. The first occurrence of that word in the document will be highlighted (**Figure 4.34**).

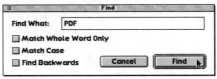

Figure 4.32 Choose Find from the Edit menu.

Figure 4.33 Enter the word you wish to find and click the Find button.

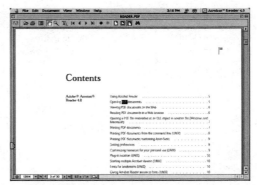

Figure 4.34 The first occurrence of that word will be highlighted.

Figure 4.35 Choose Find Again to find the next occurrence of a found word.

To find the next occurrence of a found word in a PDF document:

◆ Choose Find Again from the Edit menu (**Figure 4.35**).

The next occurrence of that word will be highlighted (**Figure 4.36**).

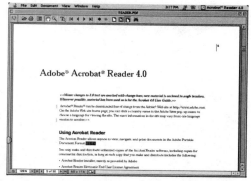

Figure 4.36 The next occurrence of that word will be highlighted.

Distributing Acrobat Reader

Adobe allows Acrobat Reader to be distributed along with PDF files, as long as all the documentation and original files are included and are not modified in any way. The original installer (Mac or Windows) must be used as the method for distributing Acrobat Reader.

To distribute Acrobat Reader on CD-ROM:

◆ Copy the Acrobat Reader Installer to the CD-ROM master. All of the original Acrobat Reader Installer files must be present.

To distribute Acrobat Reader on the Web:

◆ The best way to do this is to have a link to Adobe's Web site (www.adobe.com) or directly to the Acrobat Reader FTP site (this changes occasionally; check the current address by going to www.adobe.com first). This works better than keeping a copy on your own Web server because Adobe's version will always be current.

DISTRIBUTING ACROBAT READER

USING ACROBAT DISTILLER WITH POSTSCRIPT FILES

5

Acrobat Distiller can instantly change any PostScript file into a PDF document. PostScript files can be created directly from the Print dialog box of most applications.

The advantages of using Distiller are that it provides a few more options than Acrobat PDF Writer, it handles PostScript commands and objects better than Acrobat PDF Writer, and PostScript code is less buggy than whatever an application initially spits out when printing.

Creating PostScript Files

PostScript files are text files that consist of the exact same code that your PostScript printer gets when you print the file normally.

To create a PostScript file on a Macintosh:

1. Within any application, choose Print from the File menu.

2. Select the File option in the Destination area of the Print dialog box and click the Save button (**Figure 5.1**). This will take you to a Save dialog box so you can give the PostScript file a name and location.

3. Name the PostScript file and select a location where you want to save it.

To create a PostScript file with Windows:

1. Within any application, choose Print from the File menu.

2. Click the Print Setup button in the Print dialog box.

3. Click the Options button in the Print Setup dialog box.

4. Click the PostScript tab (**Figure 5.2**).

5. Choose the Encapsulated PostScript (EPS) option. Click OK.

6. Click OK to exit the Print Setup dialog box. Click OK in the Print Document dialog box, and the PostScript file will be created.

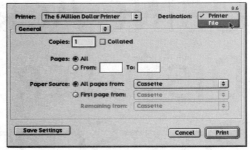

Figure 5.1 Select File from the Destination pop-up menu in the Print dialog box.

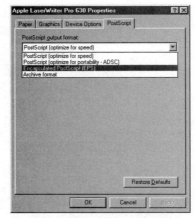

Figure 5.2 Select the EPS option in the PostScript tab of the Print Setup dialog box.

Acrobat™ Distiller™ 4.0

Figure 5.3 Double-click on the Acrobat Distiller icon.

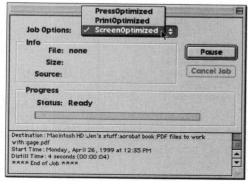

Figure 5.4 Choose a job option.

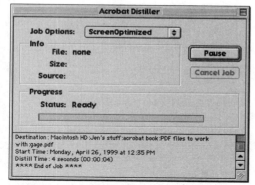

Figure 5.5 The Acrobat Distiller window.

Launching and Using Distiller

Acrobat Distiller is necessary for changing PostScript and EPS files into PDF documents.

To start Acrobat Distiller:

1. Double-click on the Acrobat Distiller icon to launch Distiller (**Figure 5.3**). This brings you to a dialog box.

2. Choose one of the Job Options, either PressOptimized, PrintOptimized, or ScreenOptimized, depending on how the image will be viewed (**Figure 5.4**). The main Acrobat Distiller window appears in the center of your screen (**Figure 5.5**).

To distill a PostScript file into a PDF file:

1. Choose Open from the File menu (**Figure 5.6**).

   The Open dialog box appears (**Figure 5.7**).

2. Select the PostScript file you wish to distill and click the Open button.

   The Save As dialog box appears.

3. Name the file in the Save as text field and click the Save button (**Figure 5.8**).

   The Acrobat Distiller window will show the progress of the distillation (**Figure 5.9**).

✔ Tip

■ You can quickly distill any PostScript file by dragging its icon on top of the Distiller icon. The file will be automatically saved in the same folder/directory of the original PostScript document and named with a .pdf extension.

Figure 5.6 Choose Open from the File menu.

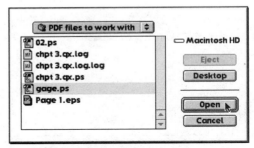

Figure 5.7 Select the file to distill.

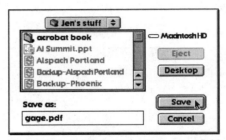

Figure 5.8 Name the file in the Save as text field.

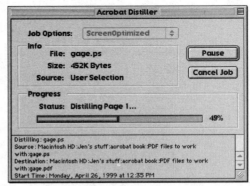

Figure 5.9 The progress bar shows the progress of the distillation.

LAUNCHING AND USING DISTILLER

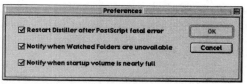

Figure 5.10 Choose Preferences from the File menu.

Figure 5.11 The Distiller Preferences dialog box.

To change Distiller Preferences:

1. Choose Preferences from the File menu (**Figure 5.10**).

The Distiller Preferences dialog box appears (**Figure 5.11**).

2. Turn any options on and off by clicking on the checkboxes.

The three different options do the following:

◆ **Restart Distiller after PostScript fatal error**. If Distiller reads code within a PostScript file that causes it to crash, it will automatically restart. This is a good option to have enabled when Distiller is being run from an unmanned server.

◆ **Notify when Watched Folders are unavailable.** If the Watched Folder is not available, a dialog box appears. Unless Distiller is being run on a server, it is a good idea to keep this option checked. Watched folders are discussed later in this chapter.

◆ **Notify when startup volume is nearly full.** Distiller uses the Startup volume as virtual memory while creating PDF files.

LAUNCHING AND USING DISTILLER

There are many more preferences in Acrobat Distiller than the tiny Preferences dialog box lets on. But instead of being labeled "preferences," they're called Job Options. These options affect the way each Distiller file is processed.

To change Distiller Job Options:

1. Choose Job Options from the Settings menu (**Figure 5.12**).

   The Job Options dialog box appears (**Figure 5.13**).

2. Select the Job Options you wish to change.

General Job Options

Changing the Compatibility setting (from 4.0 to 3.0) will allow users of Acrobat 3.0 to open and modify PDF files. However, since Acrobat 4.0 Reader is free, and file sizes are slightly smaller, Acrobat 4.0 is usually the better choice.

The Resolution setting controls the EPS image display. The Binding setting is used for facing pages.

Figure 5.12 Choose Job Options from the Settings menu.

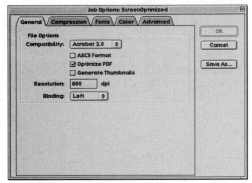

Figure 5.13 General Job Options.

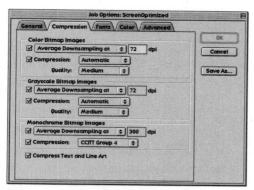

Figure 5.14 The Compression Job Options.

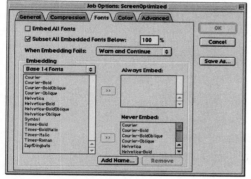

Figure 5.15 The Fonts Job Options.

Compression Job Options

The Compress Text and Line Art control provides compression for black and white draw-based artwork. The three remaining options control how different image types are compressed (**Figure 5.14**).

Choosing Downsampling reduces image resolution of those images to the dpi you specify.

Automatic or Manual Compression applies the compression you specify. This compression is lossy, meaning that the images will lose information and possibly suffer image degradation.

Both Downsampling and Automatic Compression are selected by default, and they are good options to use when you're pretty sure the PDF will be viewed only on screen.

Fonts Job Options

The Embed All Fonts option automatically embeds fonts, regardless of the contents of the Always Embed list or the Never Embed list (**Figure 5.15**).

The Subset All Embedded Fonts Below option, when checked, looks at each font used in a document. If fewer than 35% of the characters in a font are used, only the characters used are embedded, not the entire font. This can substantially reduce the size of PDF files.

The pop-up choices for When Embedding Fails are to: Ignore, Warn and Continue, or Cancel job.

Color Job Options

The Color Job Options tab (**Figure 5.16**) offers a variety of settings that apply if you plan on printing the PDF file.

The settings you see when you access this area are the ones that are the best to use when PDF files are to be displayed only on screen. The three areas you can change are Conversion, Assumed Profiles, and Options.

In the Conversion area, you can choose to leave the color unchanged, convert everything for color management, convert only images for color management, or convert all colors to CalRGB (which is best for on screen viewing).

If you have chosen the option: Convert for Color Management or Convert All Colors to sRGB/CalRGB, you'll need to choose an Assumed Profiles option for each color space. The Assumed Profiles area lets you calibrate the three areas: Gray, RGB, and CMYK.

The last area lets you check or uncheck a variety of Options. You can check or uncheck: Preserve Overprint Settings, Preserve Under Color Removal and Black Generation, Preserve Transfer Functions, and Preserve Halftone Information.

Advanced Job Options

The Advanced Job Options tab (**Figure 5.17**) contains several settings that primarily apply if you plan on printing the PDF file at some point in the future.

The settings shown are the best choices to use when PDF files are to be displayed only on screen.

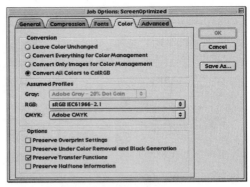

Figure 5.16 The Color Job Options.

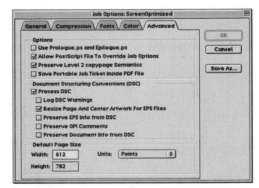

Figure 5.17 The Advanced Job Options.

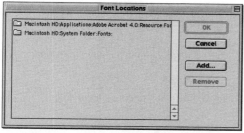

Figure 5.18 Choose Font Locations from the Settings menu.

Figure 5.19 The Font Locations dialog box.

Distiller looks for fonts in the standard font folder/directory. If you're using any font management software like ATM Deluxe, your fonts may reside in several different folders. If this is the case, you'll have to add the new locations by choosing Font Locations from the Settings menu or Command L/Control L to access the Font Locations dialog box. In this dialog box you can add and remove font locations.

To change Distiller font locations:

1. Choose Font Locations from the Settings menu (**Figure 5.18**).

   The Font Locations dialog box appears (**Figure 5.19**).

2. Remove any font locations by selecting the font to remove and clicking the Remove button.

3. Add an unlisted folder to the Font Locations list by clicking on the Add button, and then selecting the folder to add.

   The folder will appear in the Font Locations list.

LAUNCHING AND USING DISTILLER

55

You can set up Acrobat Distiller to automatically distill PostScript files into PDF files.

If your system is on a network with a server, the server is a perfect place to install and set up Distiller to automatically create PDF files from PostScript files. If you don't have a server, Acrobat can still automatically distill your files.

There are two steps to automating Distiller. First, the Distiller application must be running. Second, PostScript files need to be placed into a "watched" folder from which Distiller converts the files.

To make a Watched Folder:

1. In Distiller, choose Watched Folders from the Settings menu (**Figure 5.20**).

   The Watched Folders dialog box appears (**Figure 5.21**).

2. Click the Add button.

3. Select the folder that you wish Distiller to watch.

4. Click the OK button.

   Whenever Distiller is running from this point forward, any PostScript files placed in the designated watched folder will be distilled into PDF files.

Figure 5.20 Choose Watched Folders from the Settings menu.

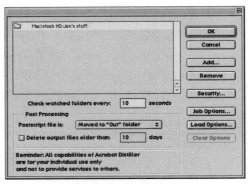

Figure 5.21 The Watched Folders dialog box.

LAUNCHING AND USING DISTILLER

EDITING AND CHANGING PDF DOCUMENTS

6

You can use PDF files immediately after you create them, but there are all sorts of things you can do to PDF files to make them more readable and easier to use. Acrobat provides several options for customizing PDF documents.

This chapter covers the changes you can make to PDF documents. Remember to save your documents after you've finished working with Acrobat so that other readers of your document will see the changes you've made. Choose Save from the File menu to save your changes to an open document, and the next time the document is opened, the changes will be there.

Starting Up and Quitting Acrobat

To run Acrobat:

◆ Locate the Acrobat icon and double-click on it (**Figure 6.1**).

   When Acrobat is loading, the Acrobat screen will appear (**Figure 6.2**), and the plug-ins that are in the Acrobat Plug-in folder will load.

To quit Acrobat:

◆ Choose Quit from the File menu (**Figure 6.3**).

   Any open documents close automatically. If changes to open documents were made, a dialog box appears asking if you'd like to save those changes.

Acrobat™ 4.0

Figure 6.1 Double-click on the Acrobat icon to run the program.

Figure 6.2 The Acrobat screen will appear while Acrobat is starting up.

Figure 6.3 Choose Quit from the File menu to exit Acrobat.

Figure 6.4 Choose Open from the File menu.

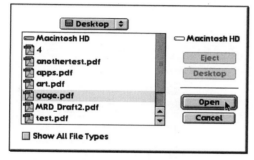

Figure 6.5 Select the file you want to open and click the Open button.

Figure 6.6 To close an open file, choose Close from the File menu.

To open a PDF file within Acrobat:

1. Choose Open from the File menu (**Figure 6.4**).

2. In the Open dialog box, select the PDF file you want to open and click the Open button (**Figure 6.5**).

To open a PDF file from the Finder (Macintosh) or from the Windows desktop:

◆ Drag the PDF file you would like to open on top of the Acrobat icon.
   or
   Double-click on the PDF file.

To close a PDF file:

◆ Choose Close from the File menu (**Figure 6.6**).
   or
   Click the close box on the document window.

Getting Information on your Document

To view Document Info:

◆ Choose General from the Document Info submenu in the File menu (**Figure 6.7**). The General Info dialog box appears.

There is all sorts of information available in the General Info dialog box. Some of this information can be changed, while other parts of the information can't be modified (**Figure 6.8**).

The items that can't be modified are:

◆ **Creator:** This is the original application that created the original document from which the PDF file was created.

◆ **Producer:** This is the software that was used to change the original document from which the PDF file was created.

◆ **Version:** This shows which version of Acrobat the document was created in.

◆ **Created:** This is the date that the PDF document was first created.

The items that can be modified, but not from the General Info dialog box:

◆ **Modified:** The last time the PDF file was changed.

◆ **Optimized:** This shows whether the file was optimized for Web use.

◆ **File Size:** The size of the PDF file; this can change as the file is modified or optimized.

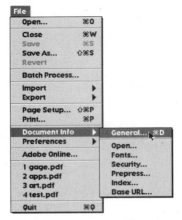

Figure 6.7 Choose General from the Document Info submenu of the File menu.

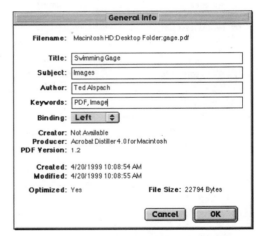

Figure 6.8 The General Info dialog box shows various information about the currently active PDF file.

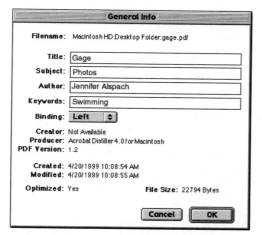

Figure 6.9 In the General Info dialog box, the Title, Subject, Author, and Keywords can be modified.

The only fields that can be changed in the General Info dialog box are the four at the top:

◆ **Title:** The title of the document, but not necessarily the title of the file. Changing the file name has no effect on the title.

◆ **Subject:** This is a descriptive category.

◆ **Author:** This is the original author of the PDF files.

◆ **Keywords:** These are words you can use for searches.

To change General Info:

1. Choose General from the Document Info submenu in the File menu.

2. Edit any of the text fields that can be edited (Title, Subject, Author, and Keywords) (**Figure 6.9**).

3. Click OK to make the changes.

4. Save the document by choosing Save from the File menu.

By default, Acrobat Reader and Acrobat open files to the first page, at the Fit Page zoom level. There may be times when you would like readers to open documents to a different page or zoom level.

To change the way files open:

1. Choose Open from the Document Info submenu in the File menu (**Figure 6.10**).

2. Make any changes in the Open Info dialog box (**Figure 6.11**).

   Those options include the Initial View, which provides the choice of viewing just the page (Page Only), the bookmarks and page, or the thumbnails and page when the document is opened. You can set the page number the document will open to in the Page text field. Set the magnification in the Magnification text field. The Page Layout style (Default, Continuous, or Facing Pages) can be set here as well.

   Window Options and User Interface Options are discussed next.

3. Click the OK button.

4. Save the document by choosing Save from the File menu (**Figure 6.12**).

   The changes will appear the next time you open the document in either Acrobat Reader or Acrobat.

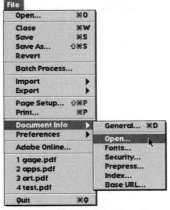

Figure 6.10 Choose Open from the Document Info submenu.

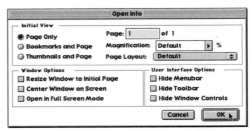

Figure 6.11 Click the OK button after you make changes in the Open Info dialog box.

Figure 6.12 Save the document after you've made your changes.

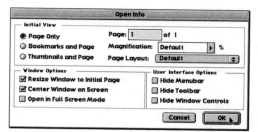

Figure 6.13 Make changes in the Open Info dialog box.

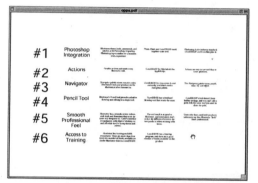

Figure 6.14 A document set to open with Menubar, Toolbar, and Window Controls hidden.

Open Info explanations

There are several things you can change in the Open Info dialog box besides the Initial View options (**Figure 6.13**).

These include Window Options and User Interface Options.

Window Options

◆ **Resize Window to Initial Page** looks at the magnification of the initial page when it is opened, and reduces the size of the surrounding window to match it.

◆ **Center Window on Screen** places the window (at whatever size) in the center of your monitor when the document is opened.

◆ **Open in Full Screen Mode** engages full screen mode, which hides the window edges, and appears to take over the entire screen.

User Interface Options

◆ **Hide Menubar** hides the menu bar (Press F7 to get the menu bar back).

◆ **Hide Toolbar** hides the Acrobat toolbar from view.

◆ **Hide Window Controls** removes the scrollbars, close, and resize boxes (**Figure 6.14**).

Manipulating PDF Pages

Occasionally, a PDF page will be rotated "the wrong way" when it is opened in Acrobat. You can change the rotation in the Rotate Pages dialog box.

To rotate a PDF page:

1. Choose Rotate Pages from the Document menu (**Figure 6.15**).

2. Select the direction you wish to rotate the pages in the Rotate Pages dialog box. Pages are rotated in 90° increments (**Figure 6.16**).

3. Select which pages are to be rotated. To rotate several sets of non-contiguous pages, you'll have to do each contiguous set separately. For instance, to rotate pages 1, 2, 7, 8 and 9 of a 10-page document, you would have to rotate pages 1 and 2 first, then pages 7, 8, and 9.

Figure 6.17 shows the original document and **Figure 6.18** shows the document after it is rotated 90° clockwise.

Figure 6.15 Choose Rotate Pages from the Document menu.

Figure 6.16 Enter the direction and the number of pages to be rotated.

Figure 6.17 The original document.

Figure 6.18 The document after being rotated 90° clockwise.

MANIPULATING PDF PAGES

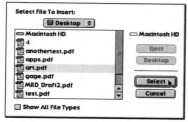

Figure 6.19 Choose Insert Pages from the Document menu.

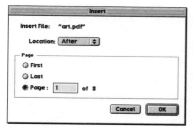

Figure 6.20 Select the file you wish to insert.

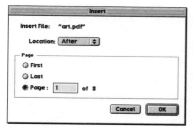

Figure 6.21 Select where the pages are to be inserted.

There really isn't a "merge" feature in Acrobat, but you do have the ability to add other PDF documents to the current, "active" PDF document.

To insert pages into a PDF document:

1. Choose Insert Pages from the Document menu (**Figure 6.19**).

2. In the Select File To Insert dialog box, find the file you'd like to insert into the current document, then click the Select button (**Figure 6.20**). The Insert dialog box appears.

3. Indicate the Location (Before or After) and the page you want to insert, then click the OK button (**Figure 6.21**).

   The pages will be inserted at the document location you selected.

✓ Tip

- If you don't want the contents of an entire PDF file to be inserted, you'll have to open that PDF file and extract the pages you want to insert. This can get confusing, so be sure to distinctly name the extracted pages of the document. Extracting pages is explained on the following page.

Selected pages from within PDF documents can be exported (Acrobat calls this extracting) into a new document. The extraction process can also be used to remove pages at the same time; this, in effect, can break a PDF document into smaller documents.

To extract a page from a PDF document:

1. Choose Extract Pages from the Document menu (**Figure 6.22**).

2. Enter the page (or pages) you wish to extract in the Extract Pages dialog box (**Figure 6.23**).

3. If you want the extracted pages deleted from the current document, check the Delete Pages After Extracting checkbox.

4. Click the OK button.

   The pages will be extracted into a new, open document. This document is not saved, so be sure to save the document before closing it (**Figure 6.24**).

Figure 6.22 Choose Extract Pages from the Document menu.

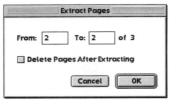

Figure 6.23 Enter the page range of pages to be extracted.

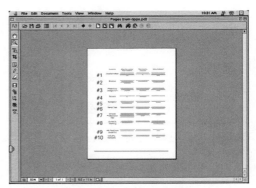

Figure 6.24 The document that has been extracted will appear in Acrobat as the current, active document.

Figure 6.25 Choose Replace Pages from the Document menu.

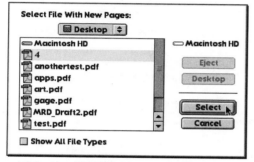

Figure 6.26 Select the file that contains the replacement pages.

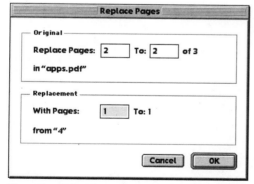

Figure 6.27 Select the page range to be replaced, as well as the page range that will replace it.

Acrobat allows you to replace a page with a PDF page from another document. This is very useful when using Adobe Illustrator (see Chapter 11) to edit individual pages of a PDF document.

To replace a page with another page:

1. Choose Replace Pages from the Document menu (**Figure 6.25**) and a dialog box comes up for you to choose the document that you want to use to replace the pages.

2. Select the file that contains the replacement pages and click the Select button (**Figure 6.26**).

3. In the Replace Pages dialog box, enter the pages to be replaced in the Original box (**Figure 6.27**).

4. Enter the replacement pages in the Replacement box.

5. Click the OK button, and your original pages will be replaced.

✓ Tip

■ You can replace any number of pages with any other number of pages. For instance, you can replace pages 4–6 in your open document with pages 11–26 from another document. The current document will then be 13 pages longer than it was before you replaced those pages.

Pages created by different applications may contain extra areas that you don't need. Acrobat provides a way to crop out the unneeded areas.

To crop a PDF page:

1. Choose Crop Pages from the Document menu (**Figure 6.28**). The Crop Pages dialog box will appear.

2. Enter the distance from each edge that you wish to crop the page in the Left, Right, Top, and Bottom boxes (**Figure 6.29**).

As you change the numbers (either by typing in new values or by clicking the arrows), a dotted line will appear on each of the margins you are cropping on the document showing you a preview of the sizes you are entering. These dotted lines show where the actual edges of the cropped page will be (**Figure 6.30**).

Figure 6.28 Choose Crop Pages from the Document menu.

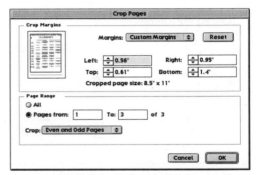

Figure 6.29 Enter where the crops will be and what pages they will affect in the Crop Pages dialog box.

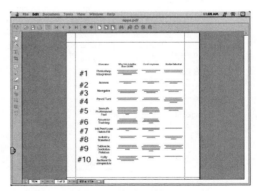

Figure 6.30 Dotted lines show where cropping will take place.

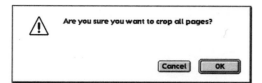

Figure 6.31 Click OK if you're sure you want to crop the pages.

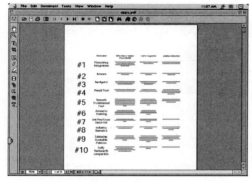

Figure 6.32 The page before cropping.

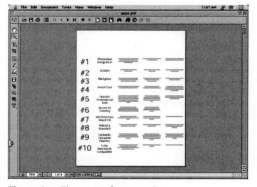

Figure 6.33 The page after cropping.

3. Enter the page range to crop. To crop all the pages in a document, choose the All radio button.

4. Click the OK button.

   A message will appear asking if you really want to crop the selected pages (**Figure 6.31**).

5. Click OK to crop the pages as you've indicated, or click the Cancel button to leave the document untouched.

   The pages will be cropped (**Figure 6.33**). You can undo this action by pressing Command-Z (Macintosh) or Control-Z (Windows) (**Figure 6.32**).

   If you save and reopen the document at a later time, there is no way to retrieve the areas that have been cropped.

Extracting removes pages from a PDF document, but it also creates a new document with the extracted pages. Sometimes you just want to get rid of certain pages. Acrobat does this with the Delete Pages command.

To delete a page from a PDF document:

1. Choose Delete Pages from the Document menu (**Figure 6.34**). The Delete Pages dialog box will appear.

2. Enter the page range you wish to delete in the Delete Pages dialog box (**Figure 6.35**).

3. Click OK to delete the pages you've specified.

   A dialog box appears asking if you're sure you want to delete the specified pages (**Figure 6.36**).

4. If you are sure, click the OK button. If not, click the Cancel button.

Figure 6.34 Choose Delete Pages from the Document menu.

Figure 6.35 Enter the page range you wish to delete.

Figure 6.36 Click OK if you're sure you want to delete the indicated page(s).

ACROBAT IN DEPTH

Acrobat has a multitude of advanced options that make PDF files easier to use and read.

These features include bookmarks, thumbnails, notes, and text editing capabilities.

All sorts of other things can be added to PDF documents as well, including links to other locations (including Web pages), and even movies! For more on Links see Chapter 8.

Acrobat is a huge piece of software. While I cover much of what it does in this and the previous chapter, Acrobat still has many other capabilities. Those features, such as Links, forms, and using the Web with PDF documents are discussed in additional chapters devoted to those specific topics. The Web features are found in Chapter 16. Chapter 12 covers the Forms feature.

Working with Bookmarks

Bookmarks are commonly used within PDF files to quickly go to a specific location (page and zoom level) within a PDF document. Bookmarks can do many other things as well, as you'll see on the next few pages.

To create a bookmark:

1. Go to a page and zoom to where you want the bookmark to go.

2. Choose Show Bookmarks from the Window menu.

3. Click on the New Bookmark icon found in the Bookmarks palette menu (it looks like a piece of paper).
   or
   Choose Create new bookmark from the Bookmarks palette pop-up menu (**Figure 7.1**).

   A new bookmark appears to the left of the document in Bookmark view. If you weren't already in Bookmark view, Acrobat changes to this view automatically.

   The bookmark is named Untitled, but the name can easily be changed (**Figure 7.2**).

4. Type the name of the bookmark. Its name could be a description of its location or the page's topic.

   Press Return after you've type the name, and the bookmark will be ready to use (**Figure 7.3**).

✓ Tip

■ If you switch from Bookmark view back to Page Only view, the bookmark will still be in place, it just won't be visible. The next time you enter Bookmark view, the bookmark(s) you've created will appear.

Figure 7.1 Choose the Create new bookmark icon from the bottom of the Bookmarks palette menu.

Figure 7.2 By default, a new bookmark is named Untitled. Its name is highlighted so that you can change the name by simply typing.

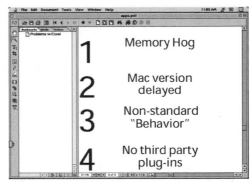

Figure 7.3 After its name is changed, the bookmark is no longer highlighted.

WORKING WITH BOOKMARKS

Figure 7.4 Change to Bookmark view by choosing Show Bookmarks from the Window menu.

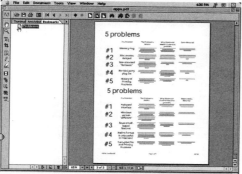

Figure 7.5 Select a bookmark by clicking on the icon to the left of the bookmark.

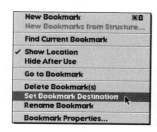

Figure 7.6 Choose Set Bookmark Destination from the Bookmarks palette pop-up menu.

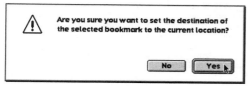

Figure 7.7 Click Yes to reset the bookmark's destination.

To view a bookmark:

1. Choose Show Bookmarks from the Window menu (**Figure 7.4**).

2. Click on the bookmark you wish to view.

   The screen changes to show the location of that bookmark.

To change the location of a bookmark:

1. Select the bookmark you wish to modify by clicking on the bookmark icon (**Figure 7.5**).

2. Move to the intended target location in the document.

3. Choose Set Bookmark Destination from the Bookmarks palette pop-up menu (**Figure 7.6**).

4. Click Yes in the warning dialog box to reset the bookmark (**Figure 7.7**).

WORKING WITH BOOKMARKS

To change a bookmark's properties:

1. Select the bookmark by clicking on its icon.

2. Choose Bookmark Properties from the Bookmarks palette pop-up menu (**Figure 7.8**).

   The Bookmark Properties dialog box appears (**Figure 7.9**).

3. Choose the type of action from the Type pop-up menu (**Figure 7.10**).

4. If you want to change the Destination as well as the type, click the Edit Destination button in the Properties palette.

5. Change the location of the bookmark by moving the page around until the bookmark is where you want it.

6. To change the Magnification setting, select a different setting from the Magnification pop-up menu (**Figure 7.11**). You can access the Magnification pop-up menu (at the bottom of the document window) even when you're inside this dialog box.

7. Click the OK button in the Bookmark Properties dialog box.

Figure 7.8 After the bookmark is selected, choose Bookmark Properties from the Bookmark palette pop-up menu.

Figure 7.9 The Bookmark Properties dialog box.

Figure 7.10 Change the Action type by choosing an action from the Type pop-up menu.

Figure 7.11 Change the magnification by clicking the Edit Destination button, and then choosing a new magnification from the Magnification pop-up menu.

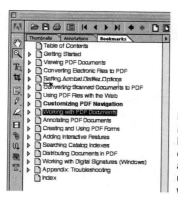

Figure 7.12
Move a bookmark by clicking on it and dragging it up or down within the list.

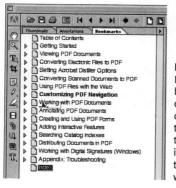

Figure 7.13
Embed a bookmark by dragging it up or down within the list and to the right of the icon you wish to embed it within.

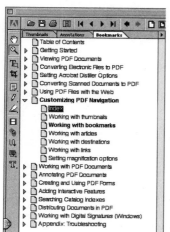

Figure 7.14
When a bookmark is embedded, it appears under and indented from the original bookmark.

By default, bookmarks appear in the order in which you create them. However, you might want to change that order, or change the long list into a more useful hierarchical approach. For instance, you may want a section page to be a main category, while a chapter opener would be a subcategory.

To change the placement of a bookmark within the list:

1. Select the bookmark to be moved by clicking on its icon.

2. Drag the bookmark up or down within the list. A black line will appear under the icon of a bookmark showing you where the dragged bookmark will be moved (**Figure 7.12**).

3. Release the mouse button. The bookmark appears in its new location.

To move a bookmark so that it is embedded hierarchically within another bookmark:

1. Select the bookmark to be embedded by clicking on its icon.

2. Drag the bookmark up or down within the list just to the right of the icon in which you want to embed it. A black line will appear under the name of a bookmark showing where the dragged bookmark will be moved (**Figure 7.13**).

3. Release the mouse button.

   The dragged bookmark is now "embedded" within the bookmark it was dragged on top of (**Figure 7.14**).

Working with Thumbnails

Thumbnails provide a quick and easy method to go to another page. You access the Thumbnails palette by choosing Show Thumbnails from the Window palette. Each thumbnail is a tiny representation of each page. Clicking on a thumbnail instantly takes you to that page at the current magnification level.

To create thumbnails for the current document:

◆ Choose Create All Thumbnails from the Document menu (**Figure 7.15**).

Thumbnails for the document will be created and displayed to the left of the document.

To view and use thumbnails in the current document:

1. Choose Thumbnails and Page from the View Menu.

   Thumbnails for the document will be displayed to the left of the document (**Figure 7.16**).

2. Click on the thumbnail that represents the page you wish to go to.

✓ Tip

■ New to Acrobat 4 is the ability to have floating Bookmarks, Thumbnails, Annotations, Signatures, Articles, and Destinations. To make a Bookmark tab a free-floating palette, just click and hold your mouse down while you drag the tab away from the group, then release your mouse button.

Figure 7.15 Choose Create All Thumbnails from the Document menu.

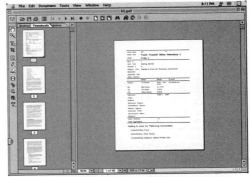

Figure 7.16 Thumbnails are shown to the left of the document.

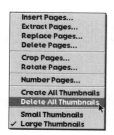

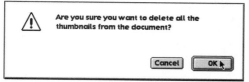

Figure 7.17 Choose Delete All Thumbnails from the Document menu.

Figure 7.18 Click OK in the warning dialog box to delete the pages.

To delete thumbnails from the current document:

1. Choose Delete All Thumbnails from the Document menu (**Figure 7.17**).

2. Click the OK button in the "Are you sure?" dialog box that appears (**Figure 7.18**).

   The document returns to Page Only view and the thumbnails are deleted.

To change thumbnails to reflect editing done within Acrobat:

1. Choose Delete All Thumbnails from the Document menu.

2. Click the OK button in the "Are you sure?" dialog box that appears.

   The document returns to Page Only view and the thumbnails are deleted.

3. Choose Create All Thumbnails from the Thumbnails palette pop-up menu.

   New, updated thumbnails for the document will be created and displayed to the left of the document.

Using Notes

Notes can add a comment or thought to a page or area on a page in a PDF document. Notes are unobtrusive and only display when double-clicked.

To create a note:

1. Choose the Note tool from the toolbar (**Figure 7.19**).

   The Note tool is now selected.

2. Create a note by dragging on a document page. The size of the rectangle created by the drag will be the size of the note (**Figure 7.20**).

   The note can be resized at any time after it is created.

   Once the mouse button is released, the note appears on the page (**Figure 7.21**).

   Type desired text into the newly created note.

Figure 7.19 Choose the Note tool from the toolbar.

Figure 7.20 Drag with the Note tool to create a note.

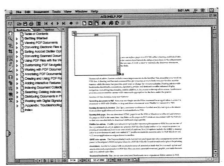

Figure 7.21 The note appears on the page.

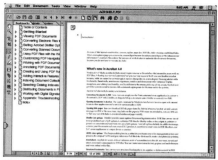

Figure 7.22 Double-click on the note to edit the text within it.

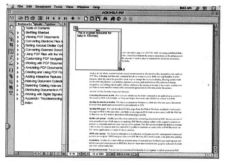

Figure 7.23 Type within the note. Resize the note by clicking and dragging in the lower-right corner.

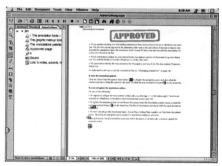

Figure 7.24 Click on the note you wish to delete

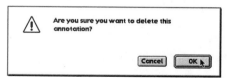

Figure 7.25 Click OK to delete the note.

To add text to an existing note:

1. Double-click on the note that you want to add text to (**Figure 7.22**).

   The note will open up, allowing you to type in text.

2. Type in the text you want to enter (**Figure 7.23**).

3. To close the note, click in the close box of the note window (in the upper-left corner of the note).

✓ Tip

- You can resize a note window by dragging the lower-right corner. The note will default to that new size when it is opened next.

To delete existing notes:

1. Click on the note you wish to delete (**Figure 7.24**).

2. Press the Delete key.

3. Click OK in the "Are You Sure" dialog box (**Figure 7.25**).

   The note is deleted.

USING NOTES

You can specify the color of notes to be one of several different colors. This is a function of pure preference; the colors don't mean anything to the note.

To change the color of a note:

1. Select the note you wish to change by clicking on it once (**Figure 7.26**).

2. Choose Properties from the Edit menu.

3. In the Note Properties dialog box, click on the Color swatch which takes you to the Color dialog box where you can change the color (**Figure 7.27**).

4. Choose a Color Picker (CMYK Picker, Crayon Picker, HLS Picker, HSV Picker, HTML Picker, or RGB Picker (**Figure 7.28**).

5. Choose a new color for your note. In this case I clicked on a crayon to choose the color I wanted.

6. Click the OK button to change the color of the note (**Figure 7.29**).

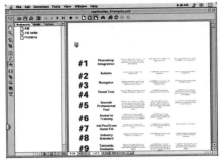

Figure 7.26 Click on the note you want to change.

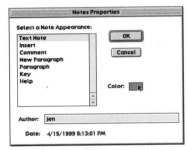

Figure 7.27 In the Note Properties dialog box, click the Color swatch to change the color using the various color pickers.

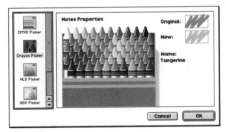

Figure 7.28 Choose a Color Picker.

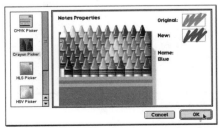

Figure 7.29 Click OK to change your note color.

USING NOTES

Figure 7.30 Choose the TouchUp Text tool from the toolbar.

Editing Text

To edit text within Acrobat:

1. Choose the TouchUp Text tool from the toolbar (**Figure 7.30**).

2. Click on any text in the PDF document.

3. Select text by dragging across it (**Figure 7.31**).

4. Replace selected text by typing.

To move text within Acrobat:

1. Choose the TouchUp Text tool from the toolbar.

2. Click on any text in the PDF document. Triangles appear to the left of the text.

3. Move the text by clicking on the triangles to the left of that text and dragging to a new location (**Figure 7.32**).

To delete text within Acrobat:

1. Choose the TouchUp Text tool from the toolbar.

2. Click on any text in the PDF document.

3. Select text by dragging across it.

4. Press the Delete key.

✓ Tip

- Double-clicking on text selects one word at a time. Clicking three times selects an entire row of text.

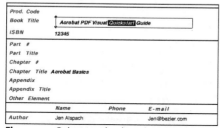

Figure 7.31 Select text by dragging across it.

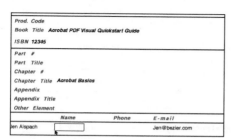

Figure 7.32 Move the text by clicking on the triangles to the left of that text and dragging to a new location.

Adding Multimedia to a PDF Document

Because PDFs can live anywhere, from screen to paper, you might want to add little "extras" that take advantage of one medium or the other. For instance, you can add movies to a document that can only be viewed when the document is viewed onscreen (that is, until someone finds a way to embed movies into paper).

To add movies to a PDF document:

1. Choose the Movie tool from the toolbar (**Figure 7.33**).

2. Drag a rectangle to indicate the size and location where you'd like a movie to be placed (**Figure 7.34**).

3. After you finish the rectangle, the Open Movie dialog box appears. Select a movie from the Open Movie dialog box.

   After you select a movie, the Movie Properties dialog box appears (**Figure 7.35**).

4. Enter any changes to the way the movie will open and play, and then click OK.

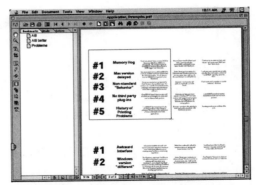

Figure 7.33 Choose the Movie tool from the toolbar.

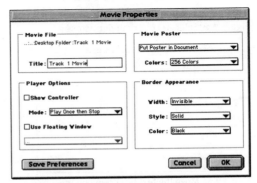

Figure 7.34 Drag a rectangle to define the size and location of the movie.

Figure 7.35 In the Movie Properties dialog box, set the way the movie opens and plays.

Figure 7.36 Choose the Article tool from the toolbar.

Creating and Using Articles

Articles allow readers to follow stories easily in PDF documents. Articles let you read related areas (like you would in a newspaper) by linking text boxes to other text boxes.

To create an article:

1. Choose the Article tool from the toolbar (**Figure 7.36**).

2. With the Article tool, click and drag around the first section of the text you want to define as part of an article (**Figure 7.37**).

When the mouse button is released, the article will be surrounded by a four-cornered box and numbered, using the scheme 1-1, where the first number is the number of the article, and the second number is the part of that article (**Figure 7.38**).

Clicking on another tool ends the article and displays the Article Properties dialog box. Here you can assign a Title, Subject, Author, and Keyword.

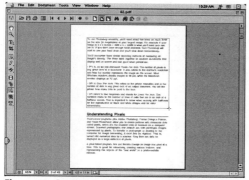

Figure 7.37 Drag around the first portion of the article.

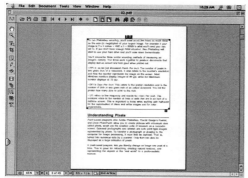

Figure 7.38 The article is indicated by a cornered box and is numbered at the top of that box.

After the first part of an article has been defined, the article can be continued to other pages or sections of text.

To continue an article:

1. Click on the original article with the Article tool.

2. A dialog box appears and asks you to click and drag out a new box. Click OK in the dialog box.

3. Drag around the next article you want linked to the first one.

   The next section of the article will continue with the second part of the number following the first article (**Figure 7.39**).

   For instance, if there were three parts to article number 1, the parts would be defined as 1-1, 1-2, and 1-3.

   Clicking on another tool ends the article, and displays the Article Properties dialog box (**Figure 7.40**). Here you can add information like Title, Subject, Author, and Keywords, or you can just click OK to leave it blank.

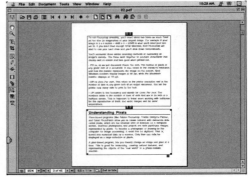

Figure 7.39 Linked articles share the same first numbers; second numbers follow in succession.

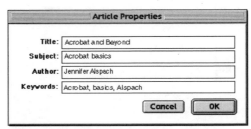

Figure 7.40 After an article has been created, information about the article can be added in the Article Properties dialog box.

LINKS

This chapter is probably as close as I'll ever get to giving golf advice, much to the appreciation of the PGA. Links in Acrobat work much like my golf game: Acrobat has the ability to instantly go to any other location, whether on the same page, the same document, a different document, or even the World Wide Web. Likewise, any golf ball I hit has a propensity to go not only anywhere on the same fairway, but could also end up anywhere on the same course, a different course, or (considering all the balls I've lost) another dimension entirely.

Acrobat provides the tools to create links that give users one click access to other locations.

How Links Work

Links provide a convenient way to navigate PDF documents. By clicking on a certain area right on the page (no bookmarks needed), the person viewing the PDF document is instantly taken to another location.

Links can be made very obvious, or they can be hidden within the document, appearing only when your cursor passes over the link.

To use a link:

◆ Click on the link that you wish to use (**Figure 8.1**).

The document instantly changes views to show the new location (**Figure 8.2**).

✔ Tip

■ You can still detect a link in a PDF document, even if it isn't displayed with an outline. When your cursor passes over the link, it will change into a pointing finger.

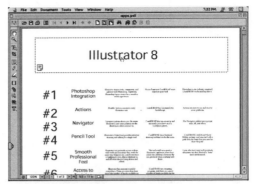

Figure 8.1 Click on a link in a PDF document.

Figure 8.2 After clicking, the document will display the linked location.

Figure 8.3 Choose the Link tool from the toolbar.

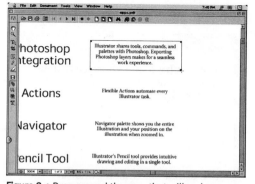

Figure 8.4 Drag around the area that will make up the link.

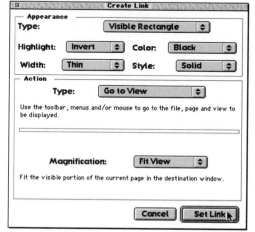

Figure 8.5 Before clicking Set Link in the Create Link dialog box, set the page and magnification at which you wish to view the link when the link is activated.

To create a link from one spot in a PDF document to another spot:

1. Choose the Link tool from the toolbar (**Figure 8.3**).

2. Drag around the area you wish to define as a link (**Figure 8.4**).

   When you release the mouse button, the Create Link dialog box appears. You might want to move this out of your way (but don't close it) when setting the location of the link.

3. Using Acrobat's tools, move to the page where you want the link to go and set the zoom level at which you wish to view the link.

4. Click Set Link in the Create Link dialog box (**Figure 8.5**).

   The link will work whenever the Hand tool is active. Test it by clicking on the link with the Hand tool.

To change zoom levels using a link:

1. Choose the Link tool from the toolbar.

2. Double-click on an existing link (**Figure 8.6**).

   When you release the mouse button, the Link Properties dialog box appears. You might want to move this out of your way (but don't close it) when setting the zoom level of the link.

3. Using the Zoom tool, zoom into the page where you want the link to zoom to (**Figure 8.7**).

4. Click OK in the Link Properties dialog box.

   The zoom level will change whenever you use the Hand tool and click on the link.

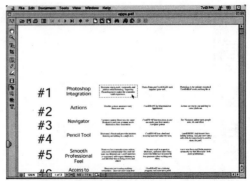

Figure 8.6 Double-click an existing link to open the Link Properties dialog box.

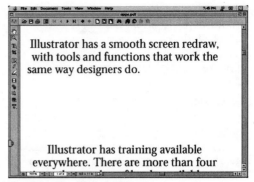

Figure 8.7 The zoomed-in view.

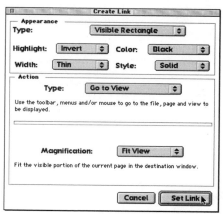

Figure 8.8 Many different properties can be changed in the Link Properties dialog box.

Figure 8.9 The different types of actions that can be assigned to a link.

To edit an existing link:

1. Choose the Link tool from the toolbar.

2. Double-click on an existing link.

   The link corners will be displayed along with the Link Properties dialog box.

3. Change the location or magnification for the link in the Link Properties dialog box.

4. Click the Set Link button in the Link Properties dialog box.

To edit the properties of a link:

1. Choose the Link tool from the toolbox.

2. Double-click on an existing link.

   The link corners will be displayed along with the Link Properties dialog box (**Figure 8.8**).

3. Change any of the actions using the Type pop-up menus in the Link Properties dialog box (**Figure 8.9**).

   You can choose from many different actions in the Type pop-up menu. You can link to a movie, a sound, a different page, an article, and more. This can be a great way to enhance your PDF document.

4. Click the Set Link button in the Link Properties dialog box.

To delete a link:

1. Choose the Link tool from the toolbox.

2. Click once on an existing link.
   The link corners will be displayed.

3. Press the Delete key.
   A box appears asking if you really want to remove the link from the document.

4. Click the OK button (**Figure 8.10**).
   The link will be removed.

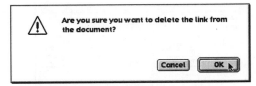

Figure 8.10 Click OK to delete the link.

USING PDFs WITH INDESIGN

Adobe built InDesign from the ground up to deal with PDF documents better than any other desktop publishing solution. At the time of this writing, QuarkXPress still cannot support importing PDF documents, and its PDF generation is weak. Adobe PageMaker, recast as the business page layout tool, has adequate PDF support, although creating PDFs still requires the use of Acrobat Distiller, a kludgy solution at best.

InDesign allows users to export entire documents as PDFs, with all sorts of information intact, including links, layers, and colors. It also supports PDF version 1.3, the newest (Acrobat 4.0-supported) PDF format for importing documents.

Importing PDF Documents into InDesign

InDesign can import PDF documents directly into InDesign documents one page at a time through the Place function.

To place PDF documents into InDesign:

1. Choose Place from the File menu (**Figure 9.1**).

   The Place dialog box appears (**Figure 9.2**).

2. Locate the PDF file you wish to import, select it, and click the Choose button. Make sure the Show Import Options box is checked.

   The Place PDF dialog box appears (**Figure 9.3**).

3. Choose the page you wish to import by clicking the little arrows under the preview and press the OK button.

   The page you chose of the specified PDF will be imported into the document (**Figure 9.4**). InDesign allows you to import one page at a time into any document.

✓ Tip

- If the Show Import Options checkbox is not checked, only the first page of the PDF file will be imported.

Figure 9.1 Choose Place from the File menu to import a PDF document into your InDesign document.

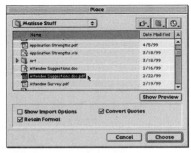

Figure 9.2 The Place dialog box allows you to choose which file to import.

Figure 9.3 The Place PDF dialog box allows you to choose which page of the PDF document to import into the document.

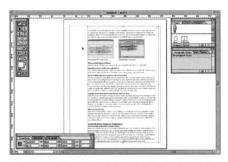

Figure 9.4 The page of the PDF file is placed in the InDesign document.

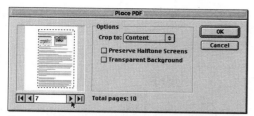

Figure 9.5 The Place PDF dialog box controls exactly how a PDF document is placed into InDesign.

Figure 9.6 The options in the Crop to pop-up menu control where the edges of the placed PDF appear.

Figure 9.7 When Transparent Background is checked, the white areas behind the actual content of the PDF document are transparent.

✔ Tip

■ The other options in the Crop to pop-up menu include Art, Crop, Trim, Bleed, and Media. These options reduce the size of the PDF to the setting specified in the original authoring application.

Import Options for PDFs

When you import a PDF into an InDesign document, you have a myriad of options to choose from (providing the "Show Import Options" checkbox is checked in the Place dialog box), including but not limited to, which page of the document you wish to import. The Place PDF dialog box (**Figure 9.5**) contains all these import options.

Page to Import: This option tells InDesign which page to import from the PDF document. Clicking the arrow-triangles at the bottom of the page allows you to move through the document a page at a time. The preview appears for each page as you click. You can quickly reach the beginning or end of the document by clicking the outermost triangle-arrows at either end of the preview.

Crop to: This option allows you to automatically reduce the size of the placed image based on the criteria you select:

> **Content:** Chosen by default, content makes the "bounding box" of the placed PDF document as large as the items in the PDF. Blank space around the outer edges of the PDF document is ignored. The options (discussed in the Tip) are shown in **Figure 9.6**.

Preserve Halftone Screens: If a halftone screen was saved with the image, this option lets it override the halftone screen setting within InDesign.

Transparent Background: This makes "empty" areas of the PDF transparent. If this option is not chosen, the background of the PDF has a white background on it. **Figure 9.7** shows a document in the Place PDF dialog box that has Transparent Background checked. This is the same document that was used in **Figure 9.5**; the main difference is that the light gray shows through the entire document now, where the background of the document was white before.

Exporting PDFs from InDesign

Any InDesign document can be exported as a PDF document using InDesign's Export function.

To export an InDesign document as a PDF:

1. Save the InDesign document you're working on.

   To save an InDesign document, choose Save from the File menu.

2. Choose Export from the File menu (**Figure 9.8**).

   The Export dialog box appears (**Figure 9.9**).

3. Choose Adobe PDF from the Formats pop-up menu.

4. Click the Save button.

   The Export PDF dialog box appears (**Figure 9.10**). It should look quite familiar to you; it's the first of the four dialog boxes from Acrobat Distiller.

5. Make any necessary changes to the options in the four sections of the Export PDF dialog box (accessible by using the Previous/Next buttons), then click the OK button.

   A PDF file will be created at this time.

Figure 9.8 Choose Export from the File menu to export a PDF from the InDesign document.

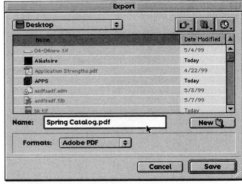

Figure 9.9 The Export dialog box allows you to name your file and to choose the format it will be exported as.

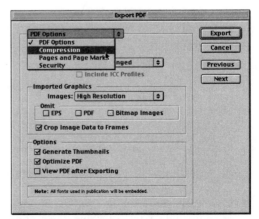

Figure 9.10 The Export PDF dialog box contains four different panels (accessible through the pop-up menu along the top of the dialog box as well as by using the Previous/Next buttons).

10

ANNOTATIONS

Acrobat ships with a variety of tools that you can use to mark up existing PDF documents. These tools include notes, stamps, file and sound annotations, and markup tools.

Annotations can be used to convey requested changes to a document, or to call out important areas within a document. In addition, you can filter out the annotations you don't want to see, so only those marked-up areas relevant to you will appear.

Types of Annotations

There are several different types of annotations in Acrobat, each with its own usefulness.

♦ **Notes:** Notes are little collapsible text areas that contain information about a specific area in a document. While notes can exist by themselves, most other types of annotations also contain (or can contain) notes (**Figure 10.1**).

♦ **Text Annotations:** Text annotations appear as text directly in a PDF. Unlike notes, they do not need to be expanded in order to be seen (**Figure 10.2**).

♦ **Audio Annotations:** These annotations contain recorded audio. Audio annotations are useful for quickly commenting on a specific area of a PDF file (**Figure 10.3**).

♦ **Stamp Annotations:** Stamps are really custom graphics that can be applied to any page in a document. Stamps can be placed on any page of any PDF document (**Figure 10.4**).

♦ **File Annotations:** Any file can be annotated to a PDF document. Sometimes it might be useful, for instance, to annotate a source file to a PDF document, or a file that contains updated or corrected information (**Figure 10.5**).

Figure 10.1 An expanded note in Acrobat is a good place to write detailed information about a specific area in a PDF document.

Figure 10.2 Text annotations are good for marking places in a PDF document that require brief notes of few words.

Figure 10.3 An audio annotation consists of a recording you create while in Acrobat.

Figure 10.4 A sample of a stamp annotation. I chose the "Draft" annotation to indicate that this PDF is not the final document.

Figure 10.5 A file annotation is a file that's embedded within an existing PDF. In this case, I've embedded the Microsoft Word file which was the source of the PDF document.

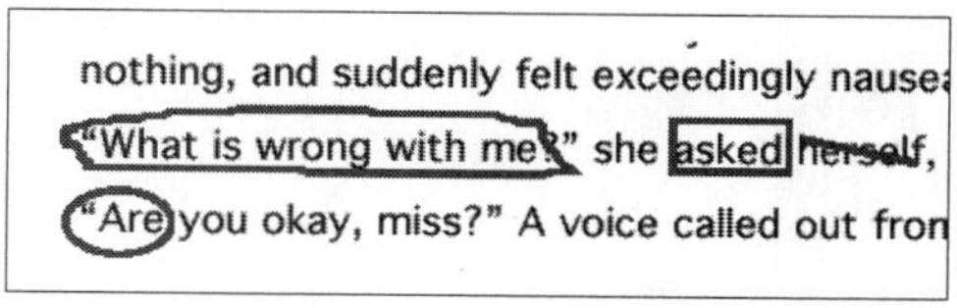

nothing, and suddenly felt exceedingly nause
"What is wrong with me" she asked herself,
"Are you okay, miss?" A voice called out fror

Figure 10.6 Multiple graphical annotations were used here to "mark up" this passage of text.

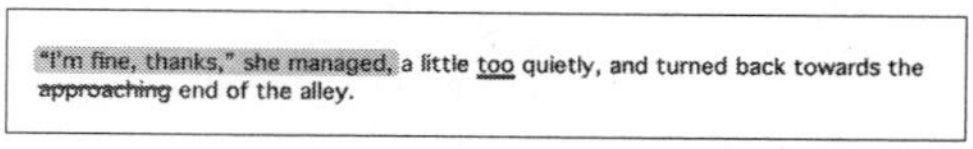

"I'm fine, thanks," she managed, a little too quietly, and turned back towards the approaching end of the alley.

Figure 10.7 Text annotation tools were used here to highlight, underline, and cross out specific areas of text.

◆ **Graphical Markup Annotations:** Acrobat allows you to create objects as annotations, such as lines, boxes, and ellipses. There's even a free-form drawing tool for custom marking (**Figure 10.6**).

◆ **Text Annotation Tools:** You may annotate specific areas of text using the Underline and Highlight annotation tools. Passages of text can be crossed out using the Strikethrough tool (**Figure 10.7**).

TYPES OF ANNOTATIONS

Notes

Notes are the most basic form of annotation. Chapter 7 contains detailed information on notes. Below is a summary of the basic usage of notes.

To create a note:

1. Choose the Notes tool (**Figure 10.8**).

2. Place the note by dragging on a document page. The size of the rectangle created by that drag will be the size of the note window (**Figure 10.9**).

3. Enter any information in the note by typing.

4. Once you've finished entering text into the note, close the note by clicking the close box on the upper-left corner of the note (**Figure 10.10**).

✔ Tips

■ Use notes to keep track of changes, to indicate changes you'd like to see in text without actually making them, and to add "hidden" information to a document that won't print.

■ You can resize the note at any time by clicking on it to display it, and then dragging the lower-right corner until the note has been resized.

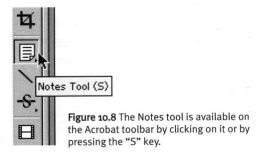

Figure 10.8 The Notes tool is available on the Acrobat toolbar by clicking on it or by pressing the "S" key.

Figure 10.9 Drag with the Notes tool to create a note of a specific size. You can always resize the note later.

Figure 10.10 Click on the close box to close the note (the icon remains after it is closed).

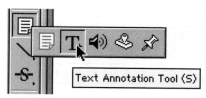

Figure 10.11 The Text Annotation tool is hidden in the same slot where the Notes tool is found.

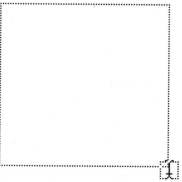

Figure 10.12 Drag with the Text tool to create a text area of a specific size. You can always resize the text area later by dragging the corners of the text area (the corners display boxes which are easy to click and drag on).

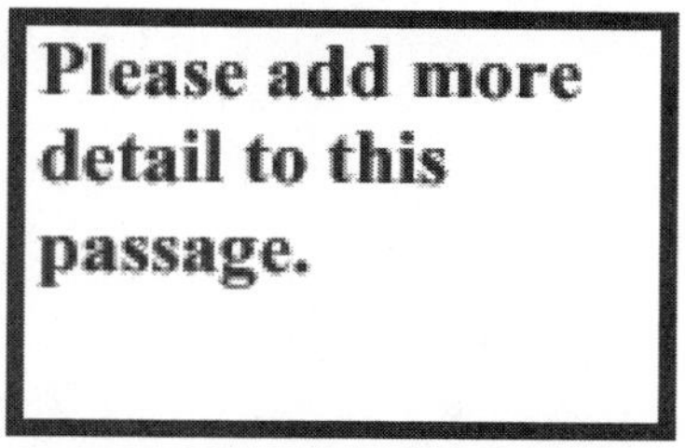

Please add more detail to this passage.

Figure 10.13 How the note appears after typing text and pressing the Enter key.

Text Annotations

Text annotations provide a method for adding straight text to a document without affecting the existing text. More "in your face" than a note, text annotations display the text directly on the document.

To create a text annotation:

1. Choose the Text Annotation tool by clicking on the Notes tool and dragging out to the right. (**Figure 10.11**).

2. Place the text annotation by dragging on a document page. The size of the rectangle created by that drag will be the size of the text window (**Figure 10.12**).

3. Enter any information to appear in the text annotation by typing. Press the Enter key when you've finished typing, and the type will appear "better" (anti-aliased) in the document. (**Figure 10.13**).

✔ Tip

- You can cycle through tools in a tool slot by pressing the Shift key in addition to the key needed to access the tool in that slot. For instance, pressing Shift-S when the Notes tool is active will cycle to the Text Annotation tool.

Audio Annotations

To add spoken commentary (or a musical interlude, if the document calls for it) to a PDF document, use an audio annotation. If your computer has a microphone, you can add any audio to a PDF easily.

To add an audio annotation to a document:

1. Choose the Audio Annotation tool (**Figure 10.14**).

2. Place the audio annotation by clicking on a document page. The Audio Annotation dialog box appears (**Figure 10.15**).

3. Click the Record button to begin recording an audio annotation.

4. Speak what you'd like to include in the audio annotation.

5. Click the Stop button when you've finished speaking. A little speaker appears on the page where your annotation was placed. (**Figure 10.16**).

   Clicking the audio annotation will play the recording.

Figure 10.14 The Audio Annotation tool is hidden in the same slot where the Notes and Text Annotation tools are found.

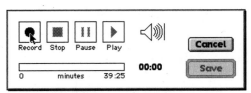

Figure 10.15 After clicking with the Audio Annotation tool, a dialog box appears which allows you to record your audio annotation.

 Figure 10.16 Audio annotations are indicated on a PDF page by a little speaker. Clicking the speaker will play the audio annotation.

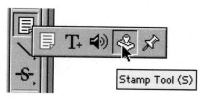

Figure 10.17 The Stamp tool is hidden in the same slot where the Notes tool, the Text Annotation tool, and the Audio Annotation tool are found.

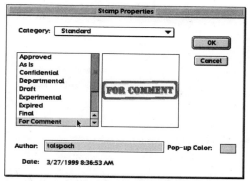

Figure 10.18 The Stamp Properties dialog box, where you can choose the type of stamp to place on the page.

much younger than her now,
be walking, but gliding. And he
ed and looked down, expecting

Figure 10.19 The stamp has been added to the document.

Stamping PDFs with Annotations

My favorite annotation is the Stamp annotation, which allows you to place custom stamp-like effects anywhere on a document. Stamp up a document as confidential, top secret, or as a working draft for your eyes only. You can even add custom stamps... anything you can create using Adobe Illustrator can be placed as a custom stamp.

To add a stamp to a document:

1. Choose the Stamp tool (**Figure 10.17**).

2. Place the stamp by dragging on a document page. Drag over an area that is as big as you'd like the stamp to be (you can always resize it later). The Stamp Properties dialog box appears (**Figure 10.18**).

3. Choose the category of the stamp you wish to use. The following pages show the stamps that are in each of the four categories that ship with Acrobat 4.

4. Choose the stamp you would like to use. You can see a preview of the stamp you've clicked on to the right of the list of stamps.

5. Click the OK button and the stamp is added to your document (**Figure 10.19**).

✔ Tip

■ If you just click with the Stamp tool, you'll place the last stamp you've selected. You can always change the stamp by Ctrl+Clicking/right-clicking on the stamp with any annotation tool.

STAMPING PDFS WITH ANNOTATIONS

Stamp Gallery

Figures 10.20-10.23 show the different stamps that can be added to a document.

✔ Tip

■ See Chapter 11: *Working with Adobe Illustrator*, to learn how to create custom stamps.

Figure 10.20 The stamps in the Standard stamp category.

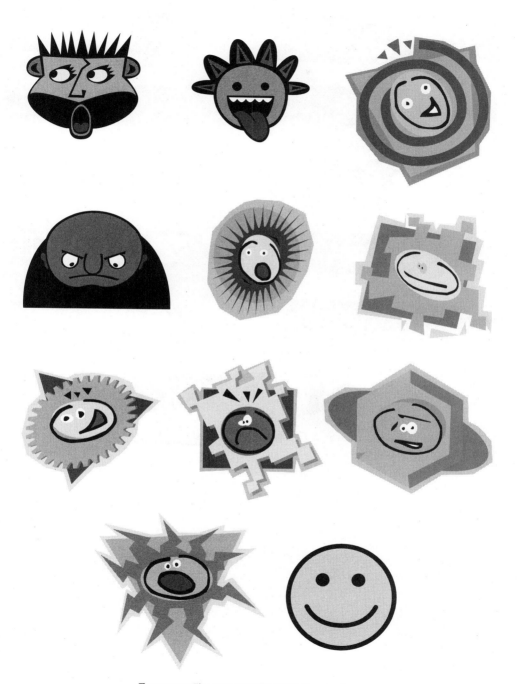

Figure 10.21 The stamps in the Faces stamp category.

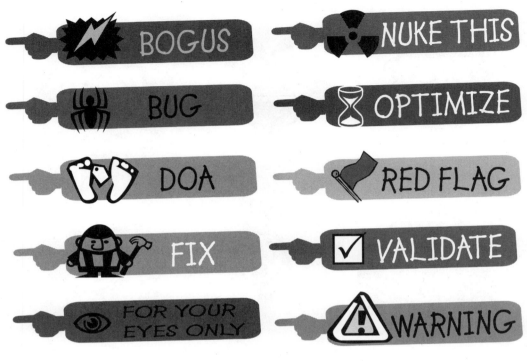

Figure 10.22 The stamps in the Pointers stamp category.

Figure 10.23 The stamps in the Words stamp category.

Creating File Annotations

File annotations are files that are attached to a PDF document. These could be any type of file, such as an image, a spreadsheet, or even another PDF file. In some cases, you might want to attach the non-PDF source file to the PDF document.

To annotate a file to a document:

1. Choose the File Annotation tool (**Figure 10.24**).

2. Click the place on the PDF document where you'd like to annotate the file. A standard "Open" dialog box appears (**Figure 10.25**).

3. Choose the file you wish to attach to the PDF document and click the Attach button. The File Annotation dialog box appears (**Figure 10.26**).

4. Choose the icon you would like to use from the list on the left, and enter any description into the Description text box, then click OK. The file will be attached to the document.

✔ Tip

- When you attach a file to a PDF document, you are *embedding* that file within the document. That means that the PDF file contains the attached file, which could dramatically increase its size. If you want to keep the PDF as small as possible, turn the original file into a PDF and add those pages to the existing PDF, providing a link to those pages in the same location where you would have placed the File Annotation.

Figure 10.24 The File Annotation tool is hidden in the same slot where the Notes tool, the Text Annotation tool, the Audio Annotation tool, and the Stamp tool are found.

Figure 10.25 A standard "Open" dialog box appears when you click with the File Annotation tool, allowing you to select the file that should be attached to the PDF document.

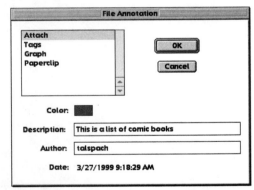

Figure 10.26 The File Annotation dialog box allows you to choose the icon that will represent this file.

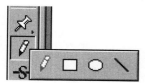

Figure 10.27
The graphical
annotation tools.

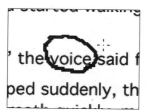

Figure 10.28 The
word "voice" has
been circled using
the Pencil tool.

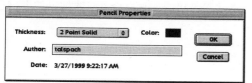

Figure 10.29 The graphical annotation tool properties
dialog boxes allow you to make changes to existing
graphical annotations. The Pencil Properties dialog
box is shown here.

Using Graphics to Mark up Pages

Acrobat has several different graphical
annotation tools, including a freeform Pencil
tool, a Rectangle tool, an Ellipse tool, and a
Line tool.

To mark up a page with the graphical annotation tools:

1. Select the tool you wish to use. The four
   graphical annotation tools share the
   same slot in the toolbar (**Figure 10.27**).

2. Click and drag on the document page to
   draw with the tool you've selected
   (**Figure 10.28**).

✔ Tip

■ You can change the color and the thick-
ness of the line used in a graphical
annotation by Control-clicking/right-
clicking on the annotation to display
annotation properties (**Figure 10.29**).

Marking up Text with Annotations

Acrobat has specific annotations to use for marking up text or individual characters. While other annotations are placed on a page near text, these annotations are tied to specific letters, numbers, or symbols. Text mark-up annotations include highlighting, underlining, and strikethrough.

To mark up text with annotations:

1. Choose the annotation tool you want to use to mark up text. The three annotation tools are hidden under the Highlighting tool (which is one of the three tools) (**Figure 10.30**).

2. Drag the tool across the text you wish to highlight/underline/strikethrough. The effect is applied to the text (**Figure 10.31**).

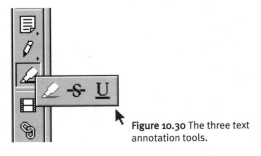

Figure 10.30 The three text annotation tools.

> "I bet you'll like it just as much," The bo
> looking innocence it held into a hideous,
> boy's mouth opened and Robin saw the

Figure 10.31 The text here has been highlighted using the Highlight Text annotation tool.

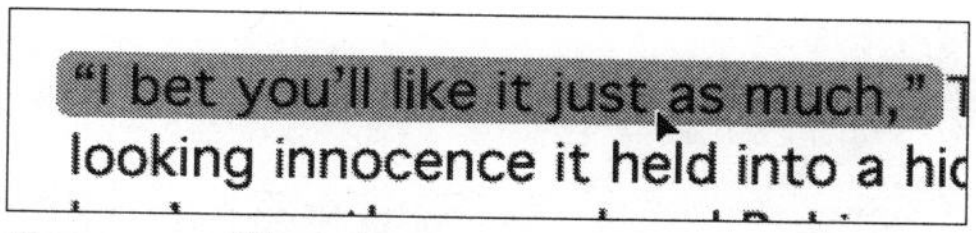

Figure 10.32 When the cursor passes over the highlighted text from Figure 10.31, the cursor changes into an arrowhead, allowing you to select the annotation by clicking.

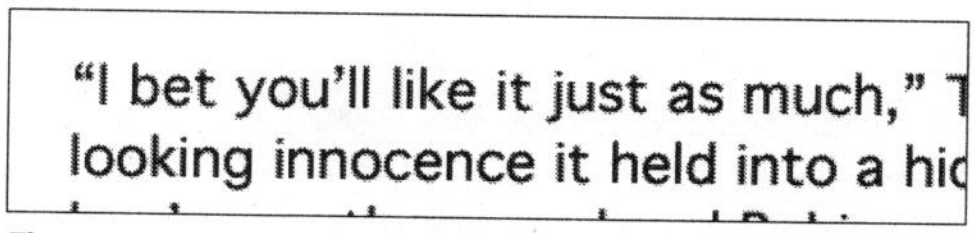

Figure 10.33 After pressing the Delete key, the text appears as it did before the annotation was applied to it.

Deleting Annotations

Any annotation can be deleted at any time. However, you need to use an annotation tool to select the annotation in order to delete it. Any annotation tool will allow you to select and delete any other type of annotation.

To delete an annotation:

1. Choose an annotation tool (it doesn't matter which one you choose, but it must be an annotation tool).

2. Click on the annotation you want to get rid of. You'll notice the cursor changes to the head of an arrow when it is over an existing annotation (**Figure 10.32**).

3. Press the Delete/Backspace key on your keyboard. After you click the OK button in a warning dialog box, the annotation will be deleted (**Figure 10.33**).

✔ Tip

■ You can delete all annotations at once by choosing Delete All from the Annotations submenu in the Tools menu.

Filtering Annotations

Once several people have marked up a document, it can be hard to determine which annotations are relevant to you. Acrobat provides a filtering mechanism that displays only the annotations that you need to see.

To filter out unneeded annotations:

1. Choose Filter Manager from the Annotations submenu in the Tools menu (**Figure 10.34**).

   The Annotations Filter Manager dialog box appears (**Figure 10.35**).

2. In the left column, uncheck the names of the people whose annotations you don't wish to view.

3. In the right column, uncheck the types of annotations you don't wish to view.

4. Click the OK button, and only the annotations you wish to view will be displayed in the document.

Figure 10.34 Choose Filter Manager from the Annotations submenu in the Tools menu.

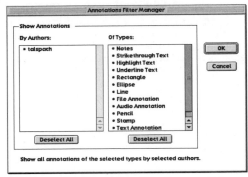

Figure 10.35 The Annotations Filter Manager dialog box.

Figure 10.36 Choose Summarize Annotations from the Annotations submenu in the Tools menu.

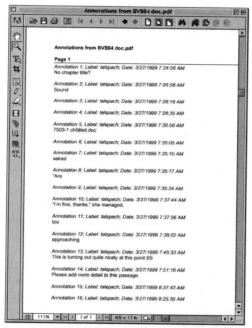

Figure 10.37 A document that was generated from the annotations I used in this document.

Summarizing Annotations

Acrobat provides a method for quickly summarizing all the annotations in an entire document. This feature actually creates a new PDF file with the annotations listed and completely documented.

To create a summary of the annotations in a document:

1. Choose Summarize Annotations from the Annotations submenu in the Tools menu (**Figure 10.36**).

   Acrobat will churn a bit if you have a large number of annotations, and then a new document appears with all annotations listed (**Figure 10.37**).

2. After you've viewed the annotations, you can either save the PDF file, print it out, or close it without saving it.

✔ Tip

■ Text that has been marked up using the text annotation tools (highlight, underline, strike through) will appear in the annotation summary file.

WORKING WITH ADOBE ILLUSTRATOR

Adobe Illustrator is the best tool you can use to edit PDF files. Illustrator is the only application that can process the multitude of graphics types and text controls that Acrobat can edit without changing them in some way, and is thus perfect to use as a complete editing tool.

In addition, you can use Illustrator to create custom stamps for Acrobat, so your logo or any vector object (or objects) can become a personalized stamp. See Chapter 10, *Annotations* for more information about applying stamps to documents.

The following pages show techniques using Illustrator 8, but the techniques will work the same whether you are using Illustrator versions 6, 7, or 8.

Working with Text and Graphics

To open a PDF file in Illustrator:

1. Choose Open from the File menu (**Figure 11.1**).

2. Select the PDF file you wish to work with from the Open dialog box and click the Open button (**Figure 11.2**).

   The Page Selection dialog box appears (**Figure 11.3**).

3. In the Page Selection dialog box, select the page you wish to open by clicking the forward and backward arrows at the bottom of the dialog box and click OK. This box will not appear if the PDF file contains only one page. Thumbnails are only present if they have been created within Acrobat.

   The document page appears in Illustrator (**Figure 11.4**).

Figure 11.1 Choose Open from Illustrator's File Menu.

Figure 11.2 Select the PDF file you wish to open.

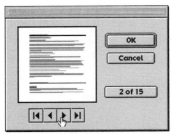

Figure 11.3 The Page Selection dialog box.

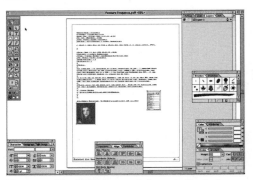

Figure 11.4 The PDF Document shown in Illustrator with all the items from the PDF selected.

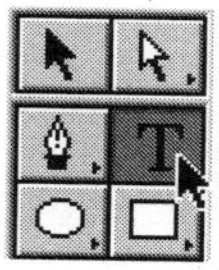

Figure 11.5 Select the Type tool in the Illustrator toolbox.

Robin's strawberry hair bounced arou
was an "extra kinky slinky" day accor
always moving up and down, like it c
quite as slinky as Tisha's. Not that R

She turned and looked down the alley
drug store on her way home from Tis
lurked in the alley. As she headed do
steps.

"What the heck am I doing?" Robin a
head. It's not like there were "things"

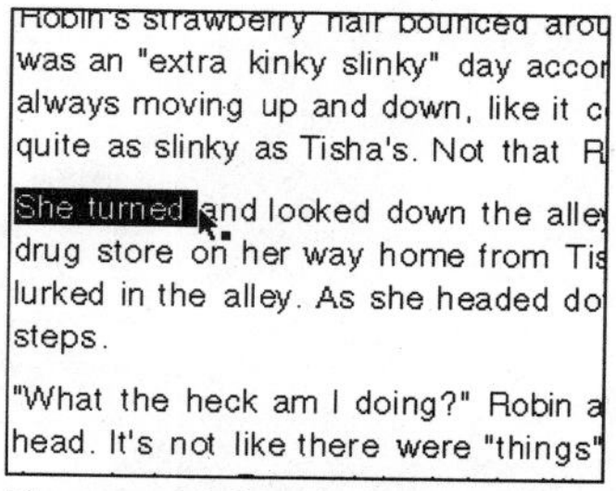

Figure 11.6 Select text by dragging the Type tool through the text.

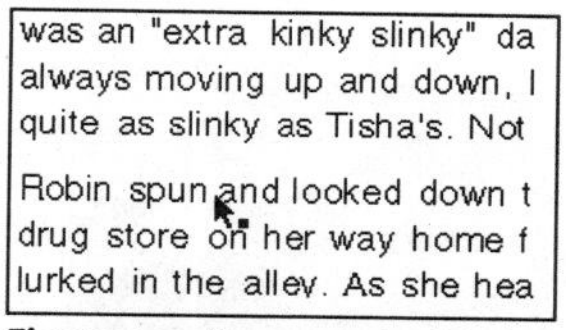

was an "extra kinky slinky" da
always moving up and down, l
quite as slinky as Tisha's. Not

Robin spun and looked down t
drug store on her way home f
lurked in the alley. As she hea

Figure 11.7 Type new text to replace the highlighted text.

To edit text of a PDF file in Illustrator:

1. Select the Type tool from the Illustrator toolbox (**Figure 11.5**).

2. Click in the area of the PDF page you wish to edit.

3. Drag to select text (**Figure 11.6**).

4. Type to replace selected text (**Figure 11.7**).

WORKING WITH TEXT AND GRAPHICS

PDF files may contain artwork in two different formats.

Pixel-based. These include photographs, scans, and images created in applications like Photoshop or Painter. You can move, scale, rotate, shear, and flip these images within Illustrator.

Vector-based. These include images created with draw and PostScript software, such as ClarisDraw and Adobe Illustrator. Also, most objects created in page layout software are vector-based. These images can be completely modified, in addition to being transformed in the same ways as pixel-based images.

To edit an image within Illustrator:

1. Choose the Selection tool (solid arrow) from the Illustrator toolbox (**Figure 11.8**).

2. Select the object or objects you wish to edit (**Figure 11.9**).

3. Select the tool or command you wish to use to edit the selected image (**Figure 11.10**).

Figure 11.8 Choose the Selection tool in the toolbox.

Figure 11.9 Select the object by clicking it.

Figure 11.10 The object after modification.

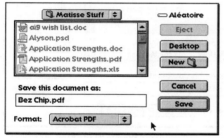

Figure 11.11 Choose Save from the File menu.

Figure 11.12 The Save As dialog box.

Figure 11.13 Choose the Acrobat PDF format from the pop-up menu.

Any file you can open in Illustrator can be saved as a PDF file, whether the file was created in Illustrator or originally as a PDF file.

To save a PDF file within Illustrator:

1. Choose Save from the File menu (**Figure 11.11**).

   The Save As dialog box appears (**Figure 11.12**).

2. Name the file and choose a location.

3. Choose Acrobat PDF format from the Format pop-up menu (**Figure 11.13**).

4. Click the Save button.

WORKING WITH TEXT AND GRAPHICS

Creating Custom Stamps

You can use Illustrator to create custom stamps for Acrobat. Since Acrobat treats PDF documents as containers for stamps, you can export an Illustrator document as a PDF page and use that page as a stamp.

To create a custom stamp in Illustrator and Acrobat:

1. Create the artwork you wish to use as a stamp (**Figure 11.14**).

2. Choose Save from the File menu.

    The Save As dialog box appears (**Figure 11.15**).

3. Name the file and select the following location to save the PDF document in:

    Acrobat 4.0/Plug-ins/Stamps

4. Choose Acrobat PDF format from the Format pop-up menu.

5. Click the Save button.

6. Open the PDF document within Acrobat.

7. Choose General from the Document Info submenu on the File menu.

    The General Info dialog box appears (**Figure 11.16**).

8. Enter the name of the Category of stamp you wish the stamp to appear under. Use a different name from the standard categories that appear by default as stamp categories (for instance, you could use the category "Fun"). Then click the OK button.

9. Choose Page Template from the Forms submenu on the Tools menu.

    The Document Templates dialog box appears (**Figure 11.17**).

Figure 11.14 Here's the Illustrator artwork I've created to use as a custom stamp within Acrobat.

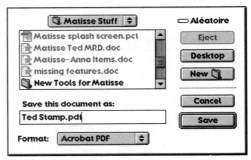

Figure 11.15 I've named the file "Ted Stamp.pdf" so I know what to look for within Acrobat.

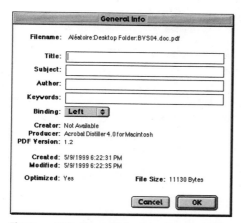

Figure 11.16 The General Info dialog box allows you to enter the name of the category of stamp you'll be using.

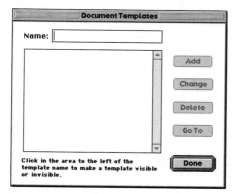

Figure 11.17 The Document Templates dialog box lets you name the stamps using a somewhat odd naming convention.

10. Type in the name of the stamp using the following convention:

CategoryName=Name

So for a category you've called "Fun" and a stamp you'd like to call "Tip" you would type in:
FunTip=Tip

11. Click the Done button.

12. Save the PDF document and close it.

The artwork can now be used as a custom stamp from within Acrobat (see the following page for details).

To use a custom stamp in a document:

1. Choose the Stamp tool (**Figure 11.18**).

2. Place the stamp by dragging on a document page. Drag over an area that is as big as you'd like the stamp to be.

   The Stamp Properties dialog box appears (**Figure 11.19**).

3. Choose the category of the stamp you wish to use. If you used "Fun" as your category, choose that one.

4. Choose the stamp you would like to use. In this case the only stamp in the category is "Chip."

5. Click the OK button and the stamp will be added to your document (**Figure 11.20**).

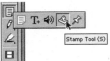

Figure 11.18 Choose the Stamp tool from within Acrobat.

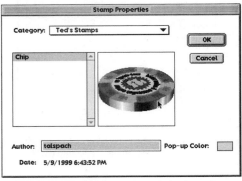

Figure 11.19 The Stamp Properties dialog box allows you to choose the stamp you wish to place in your PDF document.

Figure 11.20 The stamp has been placed in the PDF document.

12

FORMS

Interactivity. That's what electronic publishing is really all about. The 1980s theory of a paperless society is still pretty far off, for a number of reasons. One of those reasons is that electronic media had no really good means of feedback—the ability to input information in a way that a pen or pencil is used to fill out paper forms. That changed with Acrobat and its forms capabilities.

Forms allow individuals who view a document with Acrobat Reader to fill in text fields, choose options, click buttons, and even send information automatically over the Internet.

Setting up forms is designed to be as simple as possible, with a straightforward list of options and a single Form tool to assist you.

Creating Form Documents and Fields

A form document is simply a PDF file to which you can add form information. You can create a form document in any application from which you can print.

To create a form document:

1. Follow the steps outlined in Chapter 2 to create a PDF file. For this example, I've created an InDesign file in a manner very similar to the way I would create a paper-based form (**Figure 12.1**).

2. Open the file in Acrobat (**Figure 12.2**).

3. Save the file.

At this point, the document is ready to have form fields added to it.

Form Fields

Form fields are items designated for "user response." These items can be modified by anyone using Acrobat Reader 3.0 or later. The items Acrobat allows user response on are:

◆ Buttons

◆ Check boxes

◆ Combo boxes

◆ List boxes

◆ Radio buttons

◆ Text fields

In addition, you can control various elements of each of these items, including their appearance and behavior. You can even control the tab order of text fields.

You can decide what URL (Uniform Resource Locator) the information is sent to. When the user "submits" the form information, it will be sent to that location automatically.

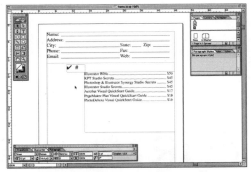

Figure 12.1 The original document in InDesign.

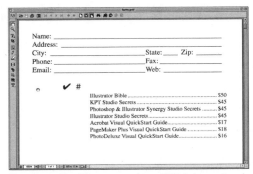

Figure 12.2 The file converted to a PDF document and opened in Acrobat.

Figure 12.3 Choose the Form tool from the toolbar.

| Name: | |
| Address: | |

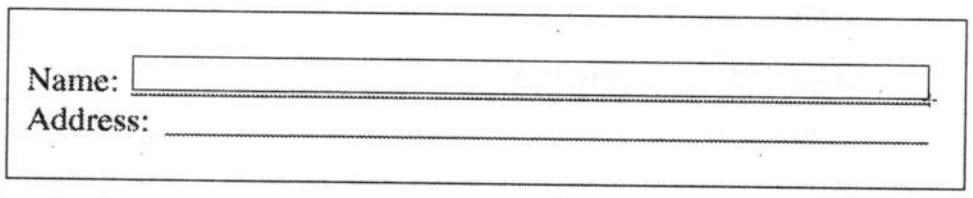

Figure 12.4 Drag with the Form tool to create a form block.

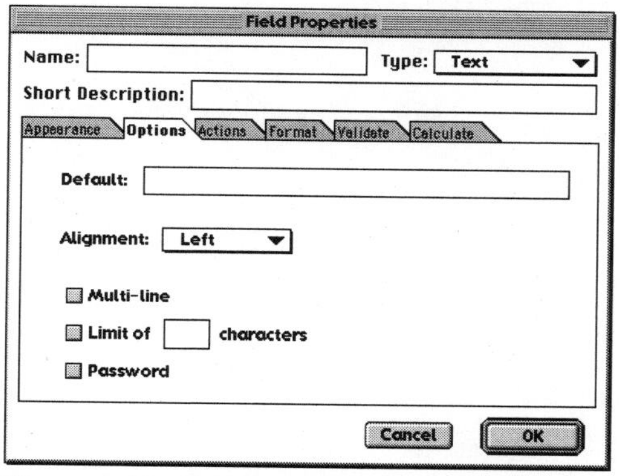

Field Properties

Name: [ ] Type: [Text ▼]

Short Description: [ ]

Appearance | Options | Actions | Format | Validate | Calculate

Default: [ ]

Alignment: [Left ▼]

☐ Multi-line
☐ Limit of [ ] characters
☐ Password

[Cancel] [OK]

Figure 12.5 The Field Properties dialog box that appears when you create a form.

URLs don't have to be just Web sites (www.site.com), they can also be FTP sites and even e-mail addresses!

Form fields are created primarily within Acrobat, although other Adobe applications such as InDesign, PageMaker, FrameMaker, and Illustrator can specify form types or destinations before the file is turned into a PDF file.

To create a form field in Acrobat:

1. Choose the Form tool from the toolbar in Acrobat (**Figure 12.3**).

2. Drag across the area you'd like to designate as a form (**Figure 12.4**). For this example, I'm creating a text field form in the "Name" area of my PDF file.

   When the mouse button is released, the Field Properties dialog box appears, showing the Text Options tab (**Figure 12.5**).

3. Change the properties (see next page) or click the OK button to use the default settings.

Field Properties Defaults

If you create a field without modifying the different options, the following default values will be in place:

◆ A text field that is flush left, contains no "dummy" text, and exists only on one line, with no border or background color.

To change the Text Options in the Field Properties dialog box:

1. In the Field Properties dialog box, click on the Options tab. Choose Text from the Type pop-up menu and the Text Options will be displayed.

2. Enter the Name of the field. Since this field is the Name in my document, I've called the field "Name." Creative, eh?

3. In the Default text field, enter any text that you would like to have appear in the field before the user activates the text field (**Figure 12.6**). I've used "Your Name Here." For a similar Name field, you might use a pretend name like "Nancy Davis" or something like "Start Typing Here."

4. Choose the alignment of the text to be entered from the Alignment pop-up menu. I've left this option the default (left aligned).

5. Check the Multi-line box if you think the information being entered may take several lines of text. This would be a good option to choose if this field were to contain all the contact information, not just Name.

6. If you want to limit the number of characters that can be entered, check the box next to Limit of, and enter the number of characters to the left of the word "characters." This is useful if the software that will be reading the data is limited to a certain number of characters.

7. Check the Password box to make the text field work as a password reader (see Chapter 15 for more about passwords).

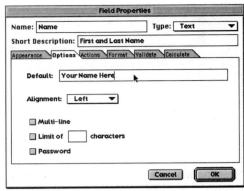

Figure 12.6 In the Default text field, enter any text that you would like to have appear in that field before the user activates it.

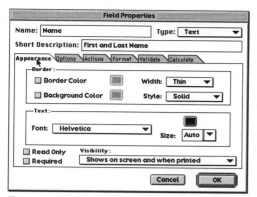

Figure 12.7 The Appearance tab in the Field Properties dialog box.

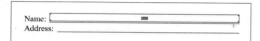

Figure 12.8 The field after being created, with the Form tool still selected.

Figure 12.9 After changing to the Hand tool, the document appears as it will look in Acrobat Reader.

To change the appearance in the Field Properties dialog box:

1. In the Field Properties dialog box, click on the Appearance tab. The Appearance options will be displayed (**Figure 12.7**).

2. If you'd like the field to have a border, check the Border Color check box and change the color by clicking on the color to the right of the check box. I left this box unchecked in my example file, since I already drew underlines in InDesign where the text would be placed.

3. If you'd like the field to have a background color that is different than the background of the file, check the Background Color box and choose a color by clicking on the icon to the right. A color picker will appear, allowing you to choose from a wide variety of colors.

4. If you've chosen to place a border or a background color on the field, you can change the width and style of it by selecting a style from the Width and Style pop-up menus.

5. Change the font of the text that will be entered by selecting a font from the Font pop-up menu. You can also modify the color and size of the font in this area.

6. Click the OK button to put your changes into effect (**Figure 12.8**).

7. Switch to the Hand tool to see how the field will look in Acrobat Reader (**Figure 12.9**).

CREATING FORM DOCUMENTS AND FIELDS

To adjust a field's position and size:

1. Choose the Form tool from the toolbar in Acrobat.

2. Click on the field you wish to modify. The handles of the field appear, and the field is surrounded by a red outline (**Figure 12.10**).

3. Click on the center of the field and drag to move the field.

   You can be more precise and accurate if you zoom in when you're adjusting (**Figure 12.11**). Press Command-Space/ Ctrl+Space to quickly access the Zoom In tool.

4. Click on the corner handles of the field to resize the field (**Figure 12.12**).

5. After you're finished, check to make sure the field is the correct size by entering sample information into it. I used my name in this example (**Figure 12.13**).

Figure 12.10 Click on the field with the Form tool to edit it.

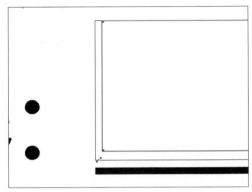

Figure 12.11 Zoom in while editing to make the field align with other objects.

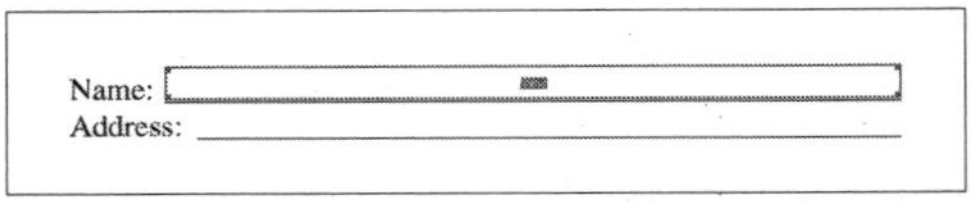

Name: _____ Address: _____

Figure 12.12 The final, resized and repositioned field.

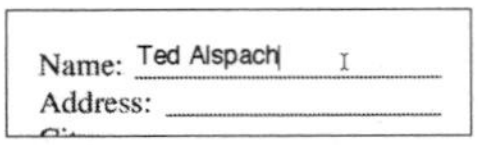

Name: Ted Alspach   I
Address: _____

Figure 12.13 Sample data entered into the adjusted field.

Figure 12.14 Option or Alt drag with the Form tool to create a duplicate of an existing field.

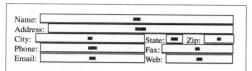

Figure 12.15 Option or Alt drag repeatedly until you've created enough duplicates.

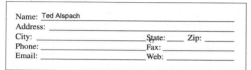

Figure 12.16 Check the appearance of the duplicated fields by switching to the Hand tool.

Instead of re-creating each field, you might find it easier to duplicate existing fields, especially if they'll be the same type of field and a similar size.

To duplicate an existing field:

1. Choose the Form tool from the toolbar in Acrobat.

2. Press the Option key for Macintosh or the Alt key for Windows, click on the field you wish to duplicate, and drag to where you'd like the new field to be (**Figure 12.14**).

3. Release the mouse button before releasing the Option/Alt key and the field will be duplicated.

4. Repeat this process until you've duplicated all the fields you need (**Figure 12.15**).

5. Switch to the Hand tool to make sure the fields look correct (**Figure 12.16**). You may need to change the sample text (which you can do with the Hand tool).

✔ Tip

■ You can press the Shift key while dragging (or Option/Alt dragging) to constrain the movement of the dragged object to a 45 degree angle. This allows for more exacting placement than by freely dragging up/down or left/right.

CREATING FORM DOCUMENTS AND FIELDS

A useful field type is the Combo Box field. This type of field lets the reader choose from several different options. The field can then be edited (or not, at your discretion). I used this field type for the State field.

To add a combo box field:

1. Choose the Form tool from the toolbar in Acrobat.

2. Drag to draw the field on the page (**Figure 12.17**).

3. In the Field Properties dialog box, choose Combo Box from the Type pop-up menu (**Figure 12.18**).

4. Enter the first value you'd like the list to show when the viewer clicks on it. In this case the list shows several state abbreviations.

5. Enter the value you'd like to send for that choice. For instance, if you wanted the state information as numbers, you could enter a number for each state. In this way each state could send back a numeric value for computation within a spreadsheet, for instance.

6. Click the Add button. That item will be added to the list.

7. Repeat Steps 4 through 6 until all the items you want in the list are added.

8. Press the OK button when finished.
   The field will look just like other fields when the Form tool is active (**Figure 12.19**). When you switch to the Hand tool, you'll be able to choose an item from the Combo Box field pop-up menu (**Figure 12.20**).

Figure 12.17 Draw the field with the Form tool.

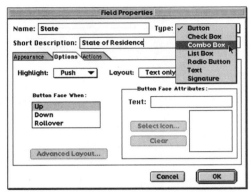

Figure 12.18 In the Field Properties dialog box, choose Combo Box as the field type.

Figure 12.19 The field (with the Form tool selected) looks just like the other fields.

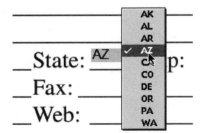

Figure 12.20 With the Hand tool selected, you can choose an item from the Combo Box field.

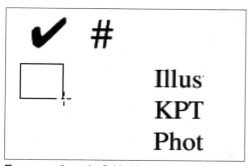

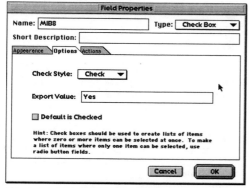

Figure 12.21 Draw the field with the Form tool.

Figure 12.22 The Check Box options.

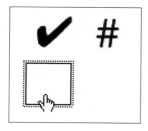

Figure 12.23 When the Hand tool is selected, the check box is initially shown unchecked.

Figure 12.24 After selecting the Hand tool, click once on the check box to see how it appears when checked.

To create a check box field:

1. Choose the Form tool from the toolbar in Acrobat.

2. Drag to draw the field on the page (**Figure 12.21**).

3. In the Field Properties dialog box, choose "Check Box" from the Type pop-up menu. The Options in the Options tab will change to represent check-box–specific options (**Figure 12.22**).

4. Name the field.

5. Choose a check style (see following page) from the Check Style pop-up menu.

6. Enter what you'd like the Export Value to be. This is the value that will be returned (next to the style name) when the box is checked. "On" is the default value, but you might find a term such as "yes" or "good" is more appropriate for your form.

7. If you'd like the field to be checked by default, check the Default is Checked check box.

8. Click the OK button.

9. Change to the Hand tool to display the check box (**Figure 12.23**). Click the box to see how it appears when checked (**Figure 12.24**).

There are several different styles of check boxes to choose from in the Options window. In addition to changing the style of the check box, you can also change the color of the check and the border.

Figure 12.25 The pop-up menu that shows the different Check Box styles.

To change check box styles:

1. With the Form tool, double-click on the field you wish to change.

2. Select a different style from the Style pop-up menu (**Figure 12.25**).
   The different styles are shown in **Figure 12.26**.

To change check box colors:

1. With the Form tool, double-click on the field you wish to change.

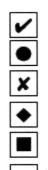

2. Click on the Appearance tab in the Field Properties dialog box (**Figure 12.27**).

3. Choose a new Border Color and Background Color. The border color is the color that "frames" the check box. The background color is the color inside the check box.

Figure 12.26 The different Check Box styles, from top to bottom: Check, Circle, Cross, Diamond, Square, and Star.

4. Choose a different Text color. This color is actually the color of the "check."

5. Click the OK button. You won't be able to see the change until you switch to the Hand tool.

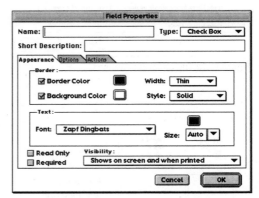

Figure 12.27 The Appearance tab for the Check Box options field type.

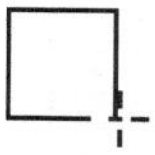

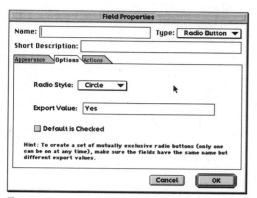

Figure **12.28** Drag to create a field with the Form tool.

Figure **12.29** The Radio Button Options screen.

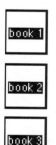

Figure **12.30** Three fields shown with the Form tool selected.

Figure **12.31** The same three fields shown with the Hand tool selected.

According to proper interface design, you should never use one radio button by itself. Therefore, the following steps show how to create one "set" of three radio buttons that work together.

To create each radio button:

1. Choose the Form tool from the toolbar in Acrobat.

2. Drag to draw a field on the page (**Figure 12.28**).

3. In the Field Properties dialog box, choose "Radio Button" from the Type pop-up menu (**Figure 12.29**).

4. Name the field and click the OK button.

5. Repeat steps 2 through 4 until there are three buttons on the page (**Figure 12.30**).

6. Select the Hand tool from the toolbar to see the fields display as radio buttons (**Figure 12.31**).

To link three radio buttons together:

1. With the Form tool, double-click on the first radio button.

2. Click on the Actions tab in the Field Properties dialog box (**Figure 12.32**).

3. Click the Add button.

4. In the Actions palette that appears, select Reset Form from the Type pop-up menu (**Figure 12.33**).

5. Click the Select fields button in the Actions palette.

6. In the Field Selection dialog box, click the Select fields button (**Figure 12.34**). The Field Selection dialog box appears.

7. Select the other radio buttons on the left, one at a time, and click the Include button (**Figure 12.35**).

8. Exit all the dialog boxes by clicking the highlighted button in each of them (OK, OK, Set Action, OK).

9. Repeat steps 1 through 8 with the other two radio buttons.

   The buttons are now linked together.

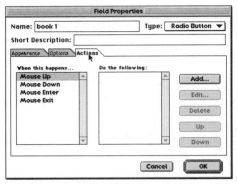

Figure 12.32 The Actions tab of the Field Properties dialog box.

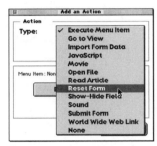

Figure 12.33 The Actions palette, showing the Type pop-up menu.

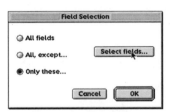

Figure 12.34 The Field Selection dialog box.

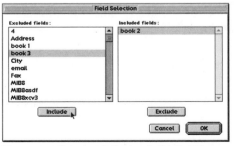

Figure 12.35 Select each field and click Include to reset those fields when the current field is clicked.

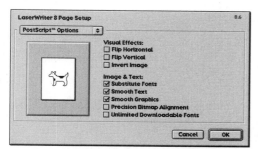

Figure 12.36 Check boxes are used in this dialog box.

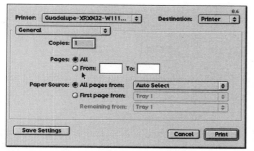

Figure 12.37 This dialog box uses a set of radio buttons.

Have you ever noticed that some functions and activities seem almost like second nature when you're choosing options within a dialog box? That's because there are certain rules that are followed in interface design. The most basic rules are those that define how certain types of objects act, and interact, with each other.

How check boxes work

Check boxes work in sets (**Figure 12.36**). Within a set of check boxes, one, none, all, or any combination may be checked ("on"). Check boxes are very flexible and independent; checking any check box usually has no effect on any other check box within that set.

How radio buttons work

Radio buttons also come in sets (**Figure 12.37**). Within a set of radio buttons, only one (and always one) of those radio buttons will be active ("on"). In that way, radio buttons are like lists or combo boxes.

How combo boxes work

Combo boxes are pop-up menus with editable text fields attached to them. The pop-up menu provides access to frequently used or common options, inserting the chosen option in the text field automatically. If the viewer wants to enter a totally different setting, they can do so in the text field.

MULTIMEDIA

The overused catchword of the 90s was indeed multimedia. Of course, a few years ago you needed a doctorate in Director in order to create anything remotely akin to multimedia. Now, fewer and fewer people are using that bloated unfriendly software, because they're using Acrobat to accomplish the same things.

Acrobat provides a simple way for you to add buttons, movies, sounds, and other "multimedia-ish" components to PDF files. This means that you can create multimedia files in any program, from QuarkXPress (with no need for "Immedia") to Adobe InDesign, Adobe PageMaker, or Adobe Illustrator.

Making Multimedia PDFs

First you'll need to prepare your PDF document for multimedia.

To set up a PDF document for multimedia:

1. Create the "background" of the screen in any software that can create PDF Files. I used a background from Adobe Illustrator for the title screen of this production.

2. Create a PDF file from the background.

3. Open the background screen document in Acrobat (**Figure 13.1**).

4. From the Document menu, choose Crop. The Crop Pages dialog box appears. If necessary, crop any excess portion of the page that appears around the edge of the screen background area (**Figure 13.2**).

   The document will then be cropped to the size you defined in the Crop Pages dialog box (**Figure 13.3**).

Figure 13.1 The document when first opened in Acrobat.

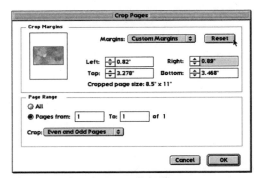

Figure 13.2 The Crop Pages dialog box.

Figure 13.3 The document after it has been cropped.

MAKING MULTIMEDIA PDFs

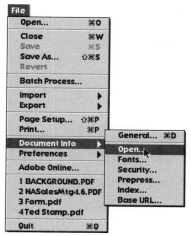

Figure 13.4 Choose Open from the Document Info submenu in the File menu.

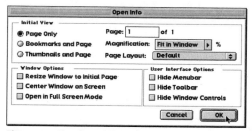

Figure 13.5 The Open Info dialog box, set up for "take control" mode.

Many multimedia presentations are totally submersive; that is, the buttons, menus, and controls within the presentation control all facets, and many times the presentation prevents the viewer from accessing standard menus and commands that they're used to in other software. In these cases, extra-special care must be taken to make the user aware of what the existing controls do and how they operate.

To have your document "take control" of the screen:

1. Choose Open from the Document Info submenu in the File menu (**Figure 13.4**). The Open Info dialog box appears (**Figure 13.5**).

2. In the Window Options area, check Open in Full Screen Mode.

3. In the User Interface Options area, select all three options: Hide Menubar, Hide Toolbar, and Hide Window Controls.

   The next time the document is opened in Acrobat or Reader, the new options will go into effect.

Considerations when hiding standard interface components

Because the people reading your document will be lacking several things they're used to, such as the menu bar and toolbar, you may want to provide options to compensate for some of the capabilities you're hiding.

For instance, a multi-page document will need navigation buttons so viewers can go to the next and previous pages. A quit or exit button can be useful. If you have a main menu, or table of contents, you might want to make a button on each page that takes you there as well.

MAKING MULTIMEDIA PDFS

Creating Multimedia Buttons

Any element can be used as a button. One setting of Acrobat's Link tool allows for just that.

To turn an existing element into a button:

1. Choose the Link tool from the toolbar (**Figure 13.6**).

2. Drag the Link tool cursor around the object you wish to use as a button. When you release the mouse button, the Create Link dialog box appears (**Figure 13.7**)

3. Choose Invisible Rectangle from the Type pop-up menu.

4. Choose Inset from the Highlight pop-up menu.

5. Choose the type of action you'd like the button to perform from the Type pop-up menu in the Action area. For this example, because I'm using the "Send" button, I've chosen the Submit Form action.

6. Click the Set Link button.

   The new button will look no different than before, and only the edges will change when you click the button with the Hand tool (**Figure 13.8**).

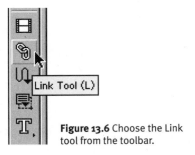

Figure 13.6 Choose the Link tool from the toolbar.

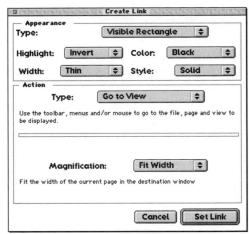

Figure 13.7 After drawing with the Link tool, the Create Link dialog box appears.

Figure 13.8 The new "button" doesn't appear any different than before it was a button.

Figure 13.9 The first button (unpushed).

Figure 13.10 The second button (pushed).

Buttons can be created as separate PDF files to give a two-part appearance to button clicking. That is, the button will look one way until it is clicked, and then it will look different after it has been clicked.

To create two different button states:

1. Create the first button state (the way the button should look before it is pushed) in any software package.

   For my example, I created a simple "go" button with bevels in Adobe Illustrator (**Figure 13.9**).

2. Create a PDF file out of the first button document.

3. Create the second button state (the way the button should look after it is pushed) in any software package.

   The second button state should be the same size as the first button state, and contain similar artwork to the first button. For my example I added a drop shadow around the first button and changed the colors of the button (**Figure 13.10**).

4. Create a PDF file out of the second button document.

   Now you're ready to add the button to an existing file.

To add a PDF button to a PDF file:

1. In the multimedia document, choose the Form tool from the toolbar (**Figure 13.11**).

2. Drag to create the area in which the button will be placed. Try to approximate the dimensions of the button you've already created as a PDF file.

   When you release the mouse button, the Field Properties dialog box appears.

3. Select the Button option from the Type pop-up menu (**Figure 13.12**). The Button Options screen appears (**Figure 13.13**).

4. In the Button Options screen, change the Highlight to Push.

5. Choose Icon only from the Layout pop-up menu, and then click the Select Icon button.

   A standard Open/Save dialog box appears.

6. Select the PDF file for the UP position of the button.

7. Click the Select Icon button in the Appearance when PUSHED area.

8. Select the PDF file for the PUSHED position of the button.

9. Click the OK button.

   When you switch back to the Hand tool, the button will display in its up view. Clicking on the button will display its pushed view.

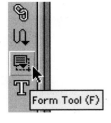

Figure 13.11 Choose the Form tool from the toolbar.

Figure 13.12 Choose Button from the Type pop-up menu at the top of the Field Properties dialog box.

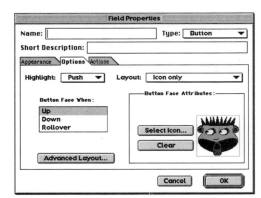

Figure 13.13 The Button Options screen showing the icon for the Up position.

CREATING MULTIMEDIA BUTTONS

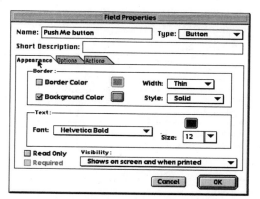

Figure 13.14 The Appearance tab of the Field Properties dialog box.

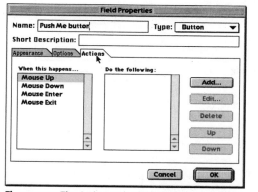

Figure 13.15 The Actions tab of the Field Properties dialog box.

Figure 13.16 The Actions palette when the Sound option is active.

Creating Hidden Multimedia Objects

Acrobat doesn't require viewers to click on something in order to get feedback. Instead, you can set up Acrobat documents so that when the cursor passes over an area, some action happens. In this example, we're creating a sound pop-up menu.

To create a non-clicking interactive area:

1. Choose the Form tool from the toolbar.

2. Drag to create the area where you want to make non-clicking interactive. The Field Properties dialog box appears.

3. In the Field Properties dialog box, choose Button from the Type pop-up menu.

4. Click on the Appearance tab (**Figure 13.14**). In the Appearance section, uncheck the Border Color and Background Color boxes.

5. Click on the Actions tab (**Figure 13.15**). Choose the Mouse Enter option in the When this happens list.

6. Click on the Add button. The Actions palette appears.

7. Choose Sound from the Type list. The Actions palette changes to display Sound options (**Figure 13.16**).

8. Click the Select Sound button and select a sound file (Acrobat can read AIFF or System 7 sounds).

9. Click OK to exit the Actions palette, and click OK to exit the Field Properties box.

   Now, when you pass over the non-clicking interactive area with the Hand tool, the sound you've chosen will play.

Automatic Events

Documents can be set up so that when a certain page is viewed, a certain activity happens. In this example a movie is played automatically when a page is viewed.

To create a movie that plays automatically:

1. Choose the Movie tool from the toolbar.

2. Click and drag to set the size of the movie.
   When you release the mouse button, the Open dialog box appears (**Figure 13.17**).

3. Choose a movie from the dialog box and click Convert.
   The Movie Properties dialog box appears (**Figure 13.18**).

4. Click OK after you've made any changes to the Movie Properties dialog box.

5. Choose Set Page Action from the Document menu (**Figure 13.19**).

6. In the Page Actions dialog box, click the Page Open item in the When this happens list (**Figure 13.20**).

7. Click the Add button.
   The Add Action palette appears.

8. Select Movie from the Type menu and click OK.

9. Click OK in the Page Actions dialog box.
   Now when the current page is displayed, the movie will play automatically.

Figure 13.17 Select a movie to be displayed in the PDF document.

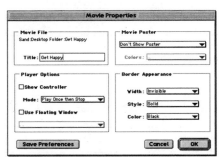

Figure 13.18 The Movie Properties dialog box.

Figure 13.19 Choose Set Page Action from the Document menu.

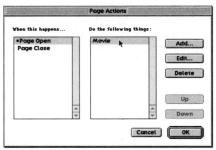

Figure 13.20 The Page Actions dialog box.

WEB CAPTURE
AND PAPER CAPTURE

14

Wouldn't it be nice to automatically convert a Web site into a PDF document, with links intact? How about converting all your paper-based documents into PDF format? Those documents could then be archived electronically and distributed via e-mail or CD-ROM. Acrobat provides a plug-in to do just that.

Acrobat lets you pull down Web pages and scan in documents that contain images, text, multiple columns, and more, while retaining links, images, colors, fonts, and other elements.

Importing Images and Scans with Capture

How Paper Capture works

Capture looks at any scanned-in artwork and text on a page and converts the text into editable text within Acrobat. In addition, the art and text placement is maintained throughout the process of capturing.

Pages are imported into Acrobat (using either the Image command or the Twain Acquire command from the Import menu) and are converted into PDF documents at that time. After they've become PDF documents, selecting Capture from the Document menu converts the document text into editable characters. The benefit of this conversion is that now the text (as characters) takes up drastically less space than a comparable scan of the same text. In addition, minor edits can be done to text within Acrobat, or the text can be heavily edited within Adobe Illustrator.

How Web Capture works

Web Capture downloads HTML-based Web pages and transforms them into PDF pages, with links and images intact.

✔ Tip

- Acrobat Capture is a stand-alone product designed to be used in conjunction with Acrobat. Acrobat 4.0 includes an Acrobat plug-in that provides most of the features in the stand-alone product, but without Capture's Batch-scanning capabilities. Batch scanning allows you to scan multiple documents all at one time.

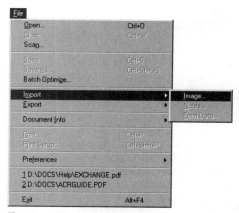

Figure 14.1 Choose Image from the Import submenu in the File menu.

Figure 14.2 The Import image dialog box.

To import an image to be captured:

1. Choose Image from the Import submenu of the File menu (**Figure 14.1**).

The Import image dialog box appears (**Figure 14.2**).

2. Select the file to be imported. In this example, I'll import a file called "Textblck."

Acrobat converts the image into a PDF document.

To import a scan to be captured:

1. Choose Twain Acquire from the Import submenu of the File menu. This menu item only appears if you have a scanner installed on your computer that supports the standard Twain functions.

The scanning window for your scanner appears.

2. Select the area of the page to be scanned and click OK (scanning software varies; your scanning screen may require different procedures).

Acrobat converts the image into a PDF document.

IMPORTING IMAGES AND SCANS WITH CAPTURE

Capturing and Editing Images and Text

Once the image is imported into Acrobat, it is ready to be "captured." This process turns text into editable characters, and images into stand-alone image objects within the document.

To capture an image:

1. Choose Capture Pages from the Document menu (**Figure 14.3**).

   The Acrobat Capture Plug-in dialog box appears (**Figure 14.4**).

2. Select Current Page.

   If you have more than one page in your document, select either All Pages to capture each page or Specified Range to capture a certain range of page (i.e., pages 4–8).

3. Click the OK button.

   Various dialog boxes appear, indicating the progress of the conversion. When the conversion is finished, the document appears in captured form.

   The following figures show the PDF document prior to being captured (**Figure 14.5**) and after being captured (**Figure 14.6**).

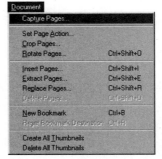

Figure 14.3 Choose Capture Pages from the Document menu.

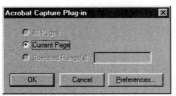

Figure 14.4 Choose which pages of the current PDF document to capture in this dialog box.

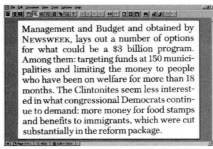

Figure 14.5 The original PDF image, showing the scanned letters. Note that this image is slightly crooked.

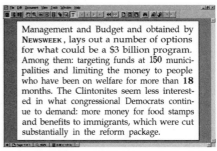

Figure 14.6 The same PDF document after being captured. The text is straightened automatically.

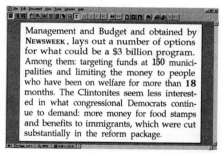

Figure 14.7 The PDF document after being captured is now ready for minor text edits.

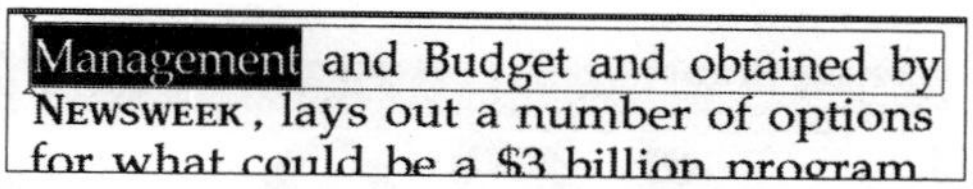

Management and Budget and obtained by
NEWSWEEK, lays out a number of options
for what could be a $3 billion program.

Figure 14.8 The word "Management" has been selected with the Text tool.

To edit captured text:

1. Choose the Text tool from the toolbar.

2. Click on the text you'd like to edit.

   Because the text is now in editable character form (**Figure 14.7**), you can change letters, spelling, and punctuation by selecting the letter to be changed and typing the new letter.

3. Double-click to select a word; drag after double-clicking to select a word at a time (**Figure 14.8**). Click and drag to select individual characters or portions of words.

4. Type in the replacement character(s).

5. Switch back to the Hand tool by choosing it from the toolbar.

Working with Suspects

Occasionally, Acrobat's Capture plug-in has trouble interpreting a word or character. When that happens, Acrobat substitutes what it thinks is probably correct, and marks the word or character as "suspect."

You can review the suspects within a captured PDF by following the steps outlined below.

To find and review suspects:

1. Choose Show Capture Suspects from the Edit menu (**Figure 14.9**).

   The Capture Suspect dialog box appears, showing the first "suspect" occurrence (**Figure 14.10**).

2. Press the Tab key to accept Acrobat's interpretation or click the Next button to find the next suspect. Pressing the Tab key will not only accept the interpretation, but will also move to the next suspect automatically. If you don't accept the suspect, you can leave the bitmapped image in place.

3. Repeat step 2 until you've reviewed all the suspect areas.

Figure 14.9
Choose Show Capture Suspects from the Edit menu.

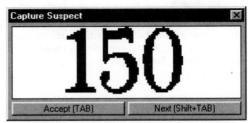

Figure 14.10 The Capture Suspect dialog box shows what Acrobat thinks should go in place of the bitmapped image area in question (in this case, the number 150).

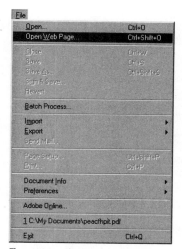

Figure 14.11 Choose Open Web Page from the File menu.

Figure 14.12 Enter the URL and click the Download button to convert the Web page into a PDF.

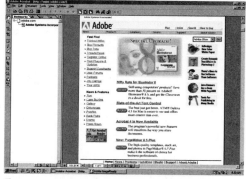

Figure 14.13 The Adobe home page in PDF form.

Converting Single Web Pages into PDF Pages

Acrobat has the ability to turn Web pages into PDF pages. If that's all it could do, it would be a useful tool. But Acrobat can turn an entire site into a single PDF document complete with active Links.

Using a 56K connection, I turned the entire "Buffy the Vampire Slayer™" site into a PDF in just a few hours. There were more than 1200 pages in the PDF, with working links throughout the document. Next, I indexed the PDF, so I could do searches for specific characters and other series information.

At work, where I have a T1 connection, I downloaded the entire Lego™ site (which is extremely graphically rich) in about an hour. More than two thousand pages, in multiple languages, which are *instantly* accessible via Acrobat and my "Lego" PDF.

To convert a single Web page to PDF:

1. Choose Open Web Page from the File menu (**Figure 14.11**). The Open Web Page dialog box appears.

2. Enter the URL of the Web page you wish to convert into a PDF document and click the Download button (**Figure 14.12**).

   The Web page begins downloading. After a few seconds (or more, depending on the page and the connection speed), the Web page appears in Acrobat as a PDF (**Figure 14.13**).

Downloading Multiple Pages and Entire Sites

Acrobat lets you control the number of levels of a Web site that you can download, from first-level (one slash in the page name) to the entire site.

Be careful when downloading an entire site, as it may be much bigger than you initially realize. In addition, many sites have more than one copy of a particular page available to speed up access to different types of users. Also, many sites have "graphically rich" versions of their sites in addition to low-end, text-heavy versions. This can quickly double the size of the site. Other sites (like the Lego site) can have multiple language versions.

You can benefit greatly by visiting the site *prior* to transforming it into a PDF document.

To convert an entire Web site to PDF:

1. Choose Open Web Page from the file menu. The Open Web Page dialog box appears.

2. Click the Get Entire Site radio button (**Figure 14.14**).

3. Enter the URL of the Web site you wish to convert into a PDF document and click the Download button.

   The Web site begins downloading. Eventually, the Web site appears in Acrobat as a PDF (**Figure 14.15**).

Figure 14.14 Click the Get Entire Site radio button, but be aware that it could take awhile to download the target site.

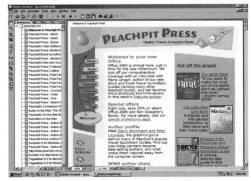

Figure 14.15 The Peachpit Press site, downloaded into a PDF.

15

SECURITY

Are you concerned that your document may fall into the wrong hands? Or maybe you'd like to distribute your document electronically, but don't want that document printed and possibly distributed to unauthorized users.

Acrobat's built-in security options can prevent unauthorized access, printing, and editing of your PDF files. Secured PDF files will stand up to rigorous attempts to bypass their password-protection schemes.

Setting Security Options

By default, PDF documents are "open," meaning that anyone can open the file, make changes to it, resave it, copy text and images from it, and work with the file as their own. You must manually add security options to a PDF document.

To prevent unauthorized opening of a document:

1. Open the document you wish to protect in Acrobat.

2. Choose Save As from the File menu (**Figure 15.1**).

   The Save As dialog box appears.

3. Choose Standard from the Security pop-up menu at the bottom of the dialog box (**Figure 15.2**).

   The Security Options dialog box appears.

4. Enter a password in the Open the Document text field (**Figure 15.3**).

5. Click the OK button.

   The Confirm Password dialog box appears (**Figure 15.4**).

6. Type in the same exact password again, and click OK.

7. Click the Save button.

   At this point the document is locked. If you close the document now, the only way it can be reopened is by supplying the correct password.

✓ Tip

■ Acrobat has no limit on the number of characters you can type, but it is case-sensitive. For instance, I password protected a document with the first verse of the theme from Gilligan's Island ("Now sit right back and you'll hear a tale…"), complete with punctuation and capitalization as needed.

Figure 15.1 Choose Save As from the File menu.

Figure 15.2 Choose Standard from the Security pop-up menu in the Save As dialog box.

Figure 15.3 Enter a password in the Open the Document text field.

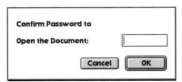

Figure 15.4 Confirm your password by retyping it in this dialog box.

Figure 15.5 Enter the password in order to open the password-protected document.

Figure 15.6 If you enter the wrong password, click the OK button to try again. If you enter the wrong password three times, you'll have to reopen the document.

To open a locked PDF file:

1. Double-click on the file, or select it from the Open dialog box within Acrobat.

   The Password dialog box appears, notifying you that the document you are trying to open is protected by a password (**Figure 15.5**).

2. Enter the password and click the OK button to open the document.

   If you enter the correct password, the document will open.

   If you enter the wrong password, the Incorrect password box appears (**Figure 15.6**).

3. If you encounter the Incorrect password dialog box, click the OK button.

4. Enter the correct password and click the OK button.

   After a wrong password has been entered three times, the dialog box ceases to appear, and the document must be opened again by double-clicking its icon or using the Open dialog box of Acrobat.

✓ Tip

■ You can easily change the "Open the Document" password of a locked PDF document. Open the document (using the current password), choose Save As, and type a new password in the Security Options dialog box. If you don't enter a password there, the password protection will be removed entirely.

Besides the ability to prevent a document from being opened without a password, Acrobat provides several other levels of protection.

Other security options

In the Security Options dialog box (access by choosing Standard from the Security pop-up menu in the Save As dialog box), there are four other options that can be controlled (**Figure 15.7**):

◆ **Printing.** This option prevents the printing of the PDF document. The Print command in the File menu is grayed out (and Command-P for Macintosh and Control+P for Windows are disabled).

◆ **Changing the Document.** This option prevents pages from being added or removed, and document options from being changed. It also prevents security options from being modified. In addition, most of the items in the Document menu are grayed out (**Figure 15.8**).

◆ **Selecting Text and Graphics.** Checking this option prevents text and graphics from being selected. This can prevent text and graphics from being copied and pasted.

◆ **Adding or Changing Notes and Form Fields.** This option prevents Notes and Form Fields from being changed. Don't check this option in a document that contains form fields you want readers to fill out.

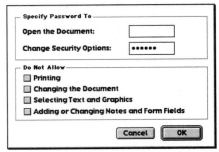

Figure 15.7 The additional options in the Do Not Allow area of the Security Options dialog box.

Figure 15.8 The Document menu with all the security options grayed out.

How to choose a password

If keeping your document secure is important, then the most important thing you can do is to have a good password. When choosing a password, keep the following rules in mind:

- **Don't Write it Down Anywhere.**
  If you can't remember it, don't use it. Writing down a password is just like duplicating a key and leaving it laying around. If you have to write it down, use some type of encoding that only you will understand, maybe something like every third character.

- **Don't pick an Easy Guesser.** What's an Easy Guesser? The name of a friend, pet, or spouse. Your social security number. A date, especially your birthday.

- **Combine Numerals and Letters.** If you use only numbers in an eight-character password, there are ten million combinations. Sounds like a lot, but a professional experienced with password decryption can zip through them quicker than you'd believe. If you use a combination of eight letters and numbers, the combinations total almost three trillion.

- **Make Your Password Easy to Remember, but Hard to Guess.**
  If someone you know can guess your password before someone you *don't* know could guess it, your password is too easy to guess. If you have to write it down, it's too hard to remember.

PDF Files
and the Web

The World Wide Web has transformed the entire world into an ugly HTML-based society of patiently waiting-for-connection Internet junkies. It wouldn't be too bad if HTML was compact, flexible, and produced good-looking content, but as we all know, that's certainly not the case.

Adobe was late in anticipating the popularity of the Web, as were Microsoft and a host of other companies. However, instead of shoring up to fight the browser wars, Adobe decided to go another route: to take its existing PDF technology and optimize it for the Web.

This chapter discusses how to use Acrobat and PDF files on the Web, from creating and displaying pages on your Web server, to reading them online.

Viewing PDFs Online with your Web Browser

PDF files can be viewed live on the Internet by Netscape and Internet Explorer Web browsers. The pages are sent one at a time, so if a reader wants to view just pages 1, 3, 16, and 243, they don't get the entire 300-page document downloaded.

Only PDF documents provided in 4.0 or 3.0 format can be downloaded one page at a time; 2.1 and older PDF files are downloaded in their entirety to the requesting Web browser.

To set up your Web browser to read PDF files:

1. Open your Adobe Acrobat folder/directory. A window appears showing its contents (**Figure 16.1**).

2. Open the Web Browser Plug-in folder/directory. A window appears that contains the PDFViewer icon (**Figure 16.2**).

3. Open your browser's folder/directory in a different window. A window appears showing its contents.

4. Drag the PDFViewer plug-in into the browser's Plug-ins folder/directory (**Figure 16.3**).

   The next time you run your Web browser, you'll be able to read PDF files with it.

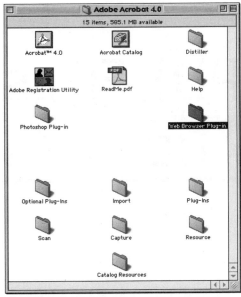

Figure 16.1 The Adobe Acrobat window. The Web Browser Plug-in folder is in the middle right of the window.

Figure 16.2 The Web Browser Plug-in window. The only item in this window is the PDFViewer plug-in icon.

Figure 16.3 Drag the PDFViewer plug-in icon into the Plug-ins folder of your Web browser.

Figure 16.4 Choose Open Location from the File menu of your Web browser.

Figure 16.5 Enter the URL in the text field.

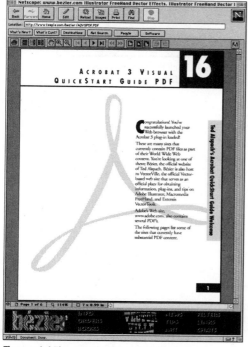

Figure 16.6 The sample page when loaded.

To view a test PDF document within your browser:

1. Launch your Web browser and confirm that you're on the Web.

2. Choose Open Location from the File menu (**Figure 16.4**).

   The Open Internet Address dialog box appears (**Figure 16.5**).

3. Enter the following into the text field, then click the OK button:

   http://www.bezier.com/AVQSPDF.PDF

   The PDF plug-in will load, and then the PDF page will be displayed (**Figure 16.6**). Acrobat Reader (or Acrobat itself, if it is on your system) will load as an application in the background, so you'll need enough free RAM to support both your browser and the Acrobat application to run at the same time.

To view any PDF documents within your browser:

1. Launch your Web browser and confirm that you're on the Web.

2. Click on any link that is a PDF file.

   Most PDF file links will have the .PDF extension after them. The document appears in your browser window.

VIEWING PDFs ONLINE WITH YOUR WEB BROWSER

Setting up PDF Files to be Viewed Online

While many Acrobat files can be read online one page at a time, not all Acrobat files can be read this way. Some Acrobat files will download the entire file before displaying the first page of the document. For Acrobat PDF files to be read one page at a time, they need to be optimized.

The process of displaying one page at a time is called byteserving. In order to make byteserving work, the PDF files need to be optimized at the time of saving.

To optimize PDF files for byteserving:

1. With the PDF file open, choose Save As from the File menu (**Figure 16.7**).

2. Check the Optimize check box in the Save As dialog box (**Figure 16.8**).

3. Click the Save button.

   The file is now ready to be placed on a Web server for downloading.

✔ Tip

■ If you make changes to your PDF file after you have done a Save As to optimize it, do not merely Save the file when you've finished making your changes. Instead, do another Save As. If you don't Save As, the optimization is removed.

Figure 16.7 Choose Save As from the File menu.

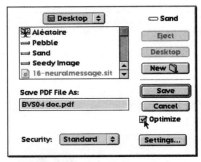

Figure 16.8 Check the Optimize check box in the Save As dialog box.

Figure 16.9 Choose Batch Process from the File menu.

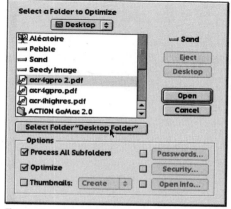

Figure 16.10 Select the folder containing the PDFs you want to optimize.

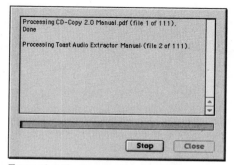

Figure 16.11 The Progress bar shows the current status of optimization.

If you have to optimize several PDF files, opening each and doing a Save As can be overly time consuming. Also, if you think you may have forgotten to optimize one PDF out of a hundred, there's no way to check, except by testing each PDF document individually.

To make tasks like this simpler, and to batch-convert PDFs created with older PDF versions into optimized 4.0 files, a batch converting utility is included as part of Acrobat.

To batch process several PDF files:

1. Within Acrobat, choose Batch Process from the File menu (**Figure 16.9**).

   The Select a Folder to Optimize dialog box appears (**Figure 16.10**).

2. Locate the folder you wish to optimize.

3. If you want to optimize all the PDFs within sub-folders/sub-directories, check the Process all Sub-Folders check box.

4. If you want to Create or remove Thumbnails in your documents, check the Thumbnails checkbox and choose the appropriate option.

   Thumbnails can substantially increase the size of PDFs, so if keeping your PDF file as small as possible is a high priority, you may want to avoid using them.

5. Click the Select Folder "Your Folder" button.

   The optimization process will begin. The Batch Operation Progress box will be displayed while Acrobat is optimizing (**Figure 16.11**).

Your Web administrator can probably tell you if your Web site is already set up to byteserve PDF files. If it isn't, explain to them that you'd like to byteserve PDF files, and they will probably be able to either upgrade their software or direct you to a Web server that has that capability.

To determine if your Web server supports byteserving of PDF files:

◆ In your Web browser, go to Adobe's Acrobat Web site which contains information on what Web servers support byteserving: `http://www.adobe.com/prodindex/acrobat/main.html`

This Web site (**Figure 16.12**) contains information on all the current server software. It also contains a generic DOS/UNIX script that may work with other software.

Currently, the oldest server software versions that support PDF byteserving are:

◆ Netscape Enterprise Server 2.0

◆ Netscape FastTrack Server 2.0

◆ OpenMarket Secure WebServer 2.0

◆ WebStar 2.0 (for Macintosh).

Check with your Internet service provider to ensure that they use one of the packages listed above (or later) or that they can install a server script on your Web server.

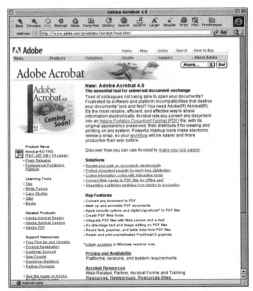

Figure 16.12 Adobe's Acrobat Web page is a good source for the latest in Acrobat information.

Figure 16.13 Choose Save As from the File menu.

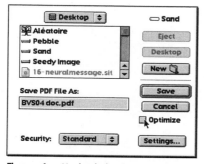

Figure 16.14 Uncheck the Optimize button in the Save As dialog box.

You can force viewers to download an entire document all at once instead of page by page. If they have an entire document on their system, they'll be able to access individual pages much faster than if they had to be downloaded individually. Of course, all the time for downloading will be there, it'll just be taken care of in one long download. To do this, you must create non-optimized files.

To remove the optimization of PDF files to prevent byteserving:

1. With the PDF file open, choose Save As from the File menu (**Figure 16.13**).

2. Uncheck the Optimize checkbox in the Save As dialog box (**Figure 16.14**).

3. Click the Save button.

   The file will now be downloaded in its entirety when viewed through or with a Web browser.

BLENDING HTML WITH PDF

17

To seamlessly combine HTML and PDF documents is actually much easier than you'd expect. Adobe has designed Acrobat with HTML integration in mind.

HTML pages can be linked to PDF pages, which can be read directly within the HTML browser. PDF pages can be embedded within HTML pages, so the PDF document appears as its own image or as a frame within an HTML page.

While Adobe has done its part to make the transition from HTML to PDF as simple as possible, there are several things you can do when creating a Web site to help your viewers jump back and forth between the two formats as transparently as possible.

Creating Links

PDF documents can contain links not only to other locations within the same PDF document, but also to locations on the Web. Likewise, HTML-based Web pages can have links within them to other HTML pages as well as PDF documents.

To create an HTML link to a PDF document:

1. In your HTML editor, type the line:

   `<A HREF="MyFile.PDF">`

   where MyFile.PDF is the name of the PDF file to which you wish to create a link.

   If MyFile.PDF is in a different directory than the current HTML file, you'll need to include that file directory path.

2. On the next line, type the words you want to use as the visible "link."

   `Click here to view my PDF document`

3. On the last line, type: `</A>`

   That tells the browser that the previous line should be underlined and indicated as a link when viewed (**Figure 17.1**).

When anyone viewing your HTML page clicks on that link, their browser will load the PDFViewer plug-in and the document will be displayed within their browser window.

If the viewing browser does not have the PDFViewer plug-in installed, the PDF file will be downloaded via FTP.

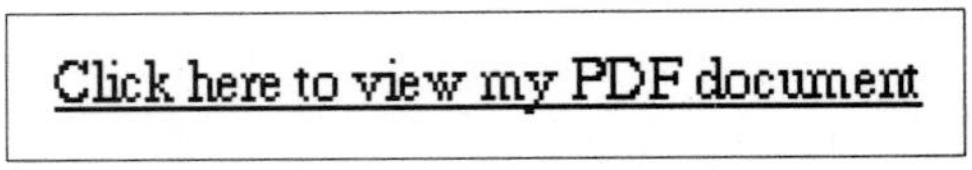

Click here to view my PDF document

Figure 17.1 This is how the link to your PDF document would appear in a Web browser such as Netscape Navigator or Microsoft Internet Explorer.

Some of the people visiting your Web site may not have Acrobat Reader 4 installed on their systems. Because of this, you may want to post a notice on your home page, or any other page that has links to PDF documents, that Acrobat 4's PDFViewer plug-in is recommended for viewing that page.

To go one step further, you may want to include a link to Adobe's FTP site so that Acrobat Reader 4 can be downloaded immediately.

To create a link for downloading Acrobat Reader 4 for Macintosh:

1. In your HTML editor, type the line:

```
<A HREF="ftp://ftp.adobe.com/pub/
adobe/acrobatreader/mac/2.x/
ardr40e.bin">
```

2. On the next line, type the words you want to use as the visible "link."

```
Click here to download Acrobat
Reader for Macintosh.
```

3. On the last line, type: </A>

That tells the browser that the previous line should be underlined and indicated as a link when viewed.

To create a link for downloading Acrobat Reader 4 for Windows 95/98 or Windows NT:

1. In your HTML editor, type the line:

```
<A HREF="ftp://ftp.adobe.com/
pub/adobe/acrobatreader/
win/3.x/ar32e40.exe">
```

2. On the next line, type the words you want to use as the visible "link."

```
Click here to download Acrobat
Reader for Windows 95/98.
```

3. On the last line, type: </A>

CREATING LINKS

Using PDF Pages on Your Web Site

Because not all of your Web site visitors will have the PDFViewer plug-in installed when they come across your Web site, there are a number of different ways to accommodate both the haves and have nots.

The best way to create a PDF-based Web site is to start with an HTML pre-home page that lets the viewer know that the primary content is PDF-based, and that they'll need PDFViewer to continue. On this page, you might also want to provide a link to a few other HTML pages on your site that contain a limited version of your site's pages.

To create a pre-home page:

1. Rename your PDF-based home page to something other than its original name (you might want to add a ".pdf" suffix).

2. Create a new HTML page.

3. In the new page, create a link to your old home page.

4. Also in the new page, create a link to another new, HTML-based page.

   This new page will contain a summary of what is on the rest of your PDF-based Web site.

5. Save the new page, naming it as your original home page.

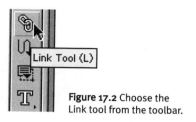

Figure 17.2 Choose the Link tool from the toolbar.

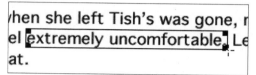

Figure 17.3 Drag around the area that will make up the link.

Figure 17.4 The URL Edit dialog box.

Individual PDF pages can be embedded within HTML pages just like JPEG or GIF images.

To embed a PDF page within an HTML page:

1. Where you'd like to embed the PDF page, type the following line:

   `<IMG SRC="MyPage.PDF">`

2. If you'd like to make the PDF document appear at 50% of the original, type:

   `<IMG SRC="MyPage.PDF" Height=50%>`

   If you enter a different percentage, the document will be scaled to that size.

To view an embedded PDF page:

1. View the HTML page that contains the PDF page. The PDF page will show up at the size you specified.

2. Click on the embedded PDF page.

   The PDF page will open in Acrobat Reader automatically at the size specified within the PDF file.

To create a link from one spot in a PDF document to a URL on the Web:

1. Choose the Link tool from the toolbar (**Figure 17.2**).

2. Drag around the area you wish to define as a link (**Figure 17.3**).

   When you release the mouse button, the Link Properties dialog box appears.

3. Choose World Wide Web Link from the Type pop-up menu.

4. Click the Edit URL button. The URL Edit dialog box appears (**Figure 17.4**).

5. Enter the URL that you'd like the link to go to, and click the OK button.

   When that link is clicked, your Web browser will start up and attempt to connect to that site.

USING PDF PAGES ON YOUR WEB SITE

18

FONT STRATEGIES

You may not consider fonts to be all that relevant to PDF documents, but they're an intrinsic part of how PDFs work.

The decision of whether and how to include fonts is critical. It affects both the size and appearance of the document.

Acrobat automatically installs Adobe Type Manager (ATM) and special "substitution fonts" during the Acrobat installation process. It is this utility and these fonts which enable you to choose not to include fonts, and still allow the document to look pretty much like the original document with the correct fonts.

In addition to this issue, there are many other font considerations to keep in mind when designing documents that will eventually end up in PDF form.

Embedding Fonts

Whenever you create a PDF document, you'll always have the option of embedding fonts into that document. Whether you do (or not) depends on several different criteria.

I've found that I choose to embed fonts more than 90 percent of the time, only choosing not to embed when I'm desperately trying to keep file sizes to a minimum. Not that fonts really add that much overhead, but 10K here and there can quickly add up to several megabytes.

When to embed

Always choose to embed fonts (via the Distiller or PDF Writer options) in the following situations:

◆ When the document is being used for proofing (appearance, not text).

◆ When the document contains text such as part of a logo that must be a certain font.

◆ When the fonts are decorative, graphical, or symbol-based (such as Zapf Dingbats or Carta).

◆ When the document needs to be used as a substitute for the original document.

◆ When the document is being sent to a service bureau or other place for final output.

The images to the right show the difference between a PDF with embedded fonts (**Figure 18.1**), and without embedded fonts (**Figure 18.2**).

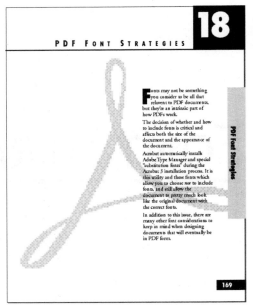

Figure 18.1 A PDF of the first page of this chapter (from the previous edition of this book) shown with fonts embedded.

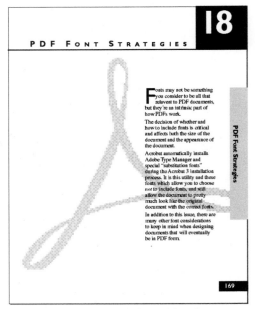

Figure 18.2 A PDF of the first page of this chapter (from the previous edition of this book) shown with fonts *not* embedded.

EMBEDDING FONTS

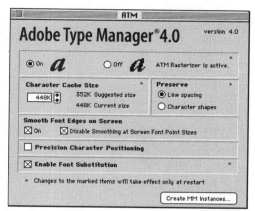

Figure 18.3 The ATM control panel.

Should Fonts be Anti-aliased?

It seems like a pretty straightforward question, but the issue of on-screen anti-aliasing is one that is sure to plague most users of Acrobat Reader. Acrobat Reader installs ATM (**Figure 18.3**), which includes the ability to anti-alias fonts. The thing is, this doesn't work just for Acrobat Reader, but also for every application on your computer.

Personally, I like the way fonts look when they're anti-aliased on screen. However, I typically use a great big 20" monitor and zoom my pages in InDesign, PageMaker, and Illustrator to at least 150%. Even standard size fonts (10 and 12 point) look pretty good when they're 15 and 18 points large in anti-aliased view. But whenever I zoom out, I have trouble reading small anti-aliased type.

Fortunately, ATM allows you to turn off anti-aliasing at smaller sizes such as 12 or 10 points. Most fonts have pre-built screen fonts at 12 points, so at this size or smaller, the fonts will not be anti-aliased.

To turn off anti-aliasing for screen font sizes:

1. Display the ATM Control Panel. Choose Control Panels from the Apple menu (Macintosh) or Start menu (Windows), and double-click on ATM.

2. Check the "Disable Smoothing at Screen Font Point Sizes" checkbox.

3. Close the ATM window.

✔ Tip

■ Anti-aliasing is the process used to make on-screen graphics and fonts look smoother. This is accomplished by making pixels along curved and diagonal edges of characters a blend of the character color (usually black) and the background (usually white).

Making the Text Fit the Column (and vice versa)

This particular issue can be a thorny one, especially since readers can't alter the column widths and font sizes of PDFs you send them.

Acrobat Reader has three useful viewing modes: Fit Page (**Figure 18.4**), in which the entire page is sized to fit within the Reader window; Fit Width (**Figure 18.5**), in which the page is sized so that the width of the page fits snugly in the Reader window; and Fit Visible (**Figure 18.6**), in which only the visible portions of the page are fit into the width of the Reader window.

All of these modes change the size of the page, but the readability of the text on the page depends on how much type there is per line. Generally, the less type per line, the more readable the text is. (Along those lines, I've made the columns in this book as narrow as possible.) The trick is to hold the reader's attention and focus from one line to the next. If lines are too long, the reader may skip a line or read a line twice, causing him or her to pause and have to reread the lines in order to make sense of the text.

In addition, if you've set up articles in your document, a reader viewing those articles will see them expand to the full width of the Reader window; if the lines of text contain too many characters, it's quite easy to become disoriented.

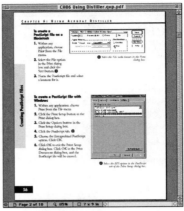

Figure 18.4 Fit Page view.

Figure 18.5 Fit Width view.

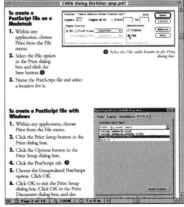

Figure 18.6 Fit Visible view.

Typefaces and Readability in PDF Documents

Type on a computer screen looks different than printed type. In order to provide the best viewing experience for readers of your PDF documents, you should constrain the use of typefaces to only those that look good on screen.

You can tell pretty easily what looks good on screen just by typing a few sentences and selecting different fonts right on your computer.

Things to avoid when choosing fonts for online viewing:

◆ **Big serifs.** Fonts which have lovely large serifs, look great when printed but terrible on a monitor; sometimes the serifs begin to resemble additional characters.

◆ **Fonts with drastically varying stroke weights.** Some fonts have vertical strokes which are nice and thick, while their horizontal strokes are thin as can be, making them difficult to read on screen.

◆ **Massively thick fonts.** If the "holes" in fonts are difficult to see on screen, they can reduce readability.

Also, try to avoid excessive tracking or kerning, and don't horizontally scale type less than 70%.

PDF and Graphics Strategies

In print publishing, enormous graphic files are the norm rather than the exception. It's all too common to provide a service bureau with a Zip cartridge so a weekly newsletter can be printed. The size of the files involved is of secondary concern to appearance, with placed images often exceeding 10Mb a piece.

However, when publishing PDF documents, size is a much larger issue. In fact, the difference between waiting just a few seconds and several minutes for something to print is measured in Kilobytes, not Megabytes. The way graphics are initially inserted and saved can dramatically change the size of a PDF document. Further, the type of graphics used can also affect the size of that document.

Using JPEG Compression

JPEG (Joint Photographic Experts Group) compression is one of the two standards of image compression, and currently the one with the most options.

Images that are compressed in JPEG format retain most of the colors (within a range of millions) in the original image, while losing a moderate amount of detail. So little detail is lost that most people outside the graphics industry can't tell the difference between the original and the modified JPEG image.

JPEG is a "lossy" form of compression, meaning that each time an image is saved as a JPEG, more of the original information is lost. Fortunately, you can have some degree of control over the amount of the image loss by choosing from various options when saving: from a limited amount of compression (and thus more original detail is maintained) to a much greater amount of compression (and less detail). Using the maximum amount of JPEG compression can reduce a file to 5% of its original size, or even less.

To set Acrobat Distiller to JPEG compression:

1. Choose Job Options from the Settings menu (**Figure 19.1**).

2. Click on the Compression tab in the Job Options dialog box (**Figure 19.2**).

3. Change the pop-up menus in the first two sections to JPEG and High.

4. Click the OK button.
   The options change to the choices you've selected. The next time you run Distiller on a file, it will use those compression settings.

Figure 19.1 Choose Job Options from the Settings menu.

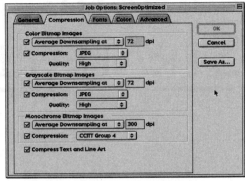

Figure 19.2 Click on the Compression tab to view the different graphics compression options.

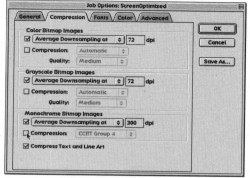

Figure 19.3 Choose Job Options from the Settings menu.

Figure 19.4 Click on the Compression tab to view the different graphics compression options. Uncheck the Automatic and Manual compression checkboxes.

Using GIF Compression

The GIF (Graphics Interchange Format) was developed by CompuServe more than ten years ago to help keep the size of online files small. The current incarnation of GIF is GIF89A, which includes the ability to have transparent areas (which can be set in any software that creates GIF89A images).

The major limitation of the GIF format is that it restricts graphics to a set number of colors, never more than 256. When cross-platform documents are being created, there are really only 216 colors that can be used (that's the number of colors that are the same between both Macintosh and Windows platforms). However, it is this limitation that allows the GIF format to be rather flexible. Instead of losing image data as with JPEG, GIF images retain each pixel's "difference" in color, but the color itself is often changed in order to fall within the limitations of the number of colors used. For monochrome images or images with only a few colors, GIF is an excellent choice.

To set Acrobat Distiller to maintain GIF image compression:

1. Choose Job Options from the Settings menu (**Figure 19.3**).

2. Click on the Compression tab in the Job Options dialog box (**Figure 19.4**).

3. Uncheck the Average Downsampling and Compression checkboxes.

4. Click the OK button.

✔ Tip

- In order to use images with GIF compression, the images must be saved as GIF images *before* they are placed into the application that creates the PDF. Acrobat has no way to convert other image types to the GIF format.

Working with Vector Graphics

One of the biggest, usually undiscovered, strengths of the PDF file format is that it can contain and maintain (not change in any way) vector graphics, such as those created with Adobe Illustrator. Vector object information is saved entirely within a PDF document; this allows the vector graphics to be displayed at any zoom level, and still maintain "perfect" quality. Another advantage of vector graphics is that using them can take up less space than an equivalent bitmap image.

Unfortunately, the opposite is also true of detailed vector graphics, especially those with large amounts of type that have been converted into outlines. In fact, when creating vector graphics for placement in PDF files, it's almost never a good idea to change type to outlines (unless some special effect needs to be applied to the text which can only be done to outlined paths). The more detail in a vector graphic, the more space it will consume (on a disk).

However, this detail can be useful if the physical size of the graphic is limited to a small amount of square inches, because Acrobat Reader can zoom in to the artwork dramatically, increasing detail.

You can keep file size to a minimum by creating PDF files from software that doesn't require you to save Illustrator documents as EPS before placing them into page layout programs. Adobe Illustrator, InDesign, and PageMaker allow you to do this.

Smaller PDFs are Better PDFs

When creating PDF documents, often the most important consideration is how to keep the size of the file as small as possible. There are a number of ways to do this, but the most effective are:

- Use as few fonts as possible. This includes limiting the use of bold and italic (and bold italic) variations of a font, as each variation is really a separate font.

- Limit the use of graphics in publications to only those that are necessary.

- Use the compression options found in Acrobat Distiller's Job Options dialog box, such as downsampling and JPEG compression.

- Use the subset option (located within the Font tab) of Acrobat Distiller's Job Options dialog box.

- Use vector graphics for large, solid areas where possible.

How Downsampling Works

Downsampling is the process of changing the resolution of any image from its placed size in a document to 72 dpi. This can dramatically decrease the size of a bitmap image, and it's an option that is enabled by default in Acrobat Distiller.

The drawback to downsampling is that when a document is viewed larger than 100%, the image will appear blocky and pixelated.

To turn off downsampling in Acrobat Distiller:

1. Choose Job Options from the Settings menu (**Figure 19.5**).

2. Click on the Compression tab in the Job Options dialog box.

3. Uncheck the Average Downsampling at checkboxes (**Figure 19.6**).

4. Click the OK button.

To turn on downsampling in Acrobat Distiller:

1. Choose Job Options from the Settings menu.

2. Click on the Compression tab in the Job Options dialog box.

3. Check the Average Downsampling at checkboxes and enter the dpi for each image (usually 72 dpi) (**Figure 19.7**).

4. Click the OK button.

Figure 19.5 Choose Job Options from the Settings menu.

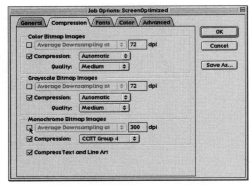

Figure 19.6 Click on the Compression tab and uncheck the Average Downsampling at checkboxes.

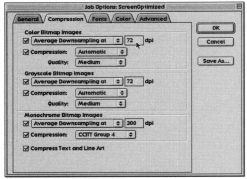

Figure 19.7 Click on the Compression tab, check the Average Downsampling at checkboxes, and enter the dpi for downsampling.

Figure 19.8 White space used in a document.

White Space

If you've ever taken an art of design class, you've probably heard your instructor rant about white space and negative space and balance and many other things which you filed away as "typical bunk."

White space is the name given by designers to, er, white space on a page. The idea behind white space is that it's a relaxing area of a page. It takes the busy feel away from the page and creates a more inviting look that is supposed to draw you in. I've never been a big fan of white space, but I do agree that filling a page up with as much text and graphics as will fit is often counterproductive.

The great thing about using white space in PDF documents is that it costs practically nothing. So what if your PDF document is 12 or 20 pages long; if the same amount of text is used, the document will be almost the exact same size. Unlike the world of printing, where adding eight extra pages to a 12-page document would cost 67% more, adding empty space to PDF documents is "free."

Take advantage of this incredibly inexpensive space by being a little more creative with your page design (**Figure 19.8**).

Backgrounds and PDF Pages

Adding solid color backgrounds to PDF pages is extremely cheap in terms of file size. In programs like Adobe InDesign, Adobe PageMaker, and QuarkXPress, solid color backgrounds take up very little extra space.

Background with tiled patterns or large, faded graphics are a different matter, however. Stay away from the complex background, as the files needed for these backgrounds can be much larger.

INDEX

A

Acrobat
- as collection of applications, 5, 7
- compatibility resolution, 3
- defined, 7
- as Director replacement, 135
- Exchange, 5
- features of, 71
- form fields creation, 123
- glossary, 7
- history of, 2–3
- HTML integration, 165
- icon, 58
- information updates from Web site, 162
- Internet, initial use of, 3
- as multimedia creation tool, 135
- PDF Writer, 5, 10–12
- quitting, 58
- running, 58
- saving changes, 58
- security, 151–55
- startup screen, 58
- user response items, 122
- viewing files online, 158–59
- and Web, 3, 157–63
- Web site, 162
- *See also* Capture; Distiller; Reader

Acrobat 4.0
- advanced Distiller options, 4
- annotations appendability, 4
- automatic bookmarking, 4
- Capture plug-in, 144
- differences, 4
- document conversion ease, 4
- "Exchange" renamed, 4
- file compression capability, 30
- Web functionality, 3
- Web page capture, 4

Actions palette, 141
active links, 3

Adobe Illustrator. *See* Illustrator
Advanced Job Options (Distiller), 54
Advance On Any Click option (Full Screen Preferences dialog box), 40
annotations
- audio, 96, 100
- deleting, 109
- file, 96, 106
- filtering out, 95, 110
- graphical markup, 97, 107
- notes, 96
- stamp, 96, 101–5
- summarizing, 111
- text, 96
- text, tools, 97, 108
- types of, 96
- use of, 95
Annotations Filter Manager dialog box, 110
anti-aliasing, 173
Apple Computer, 2
Article Properties dialog box, 84
articles
- continuing, 84
- creating, 83
- defined, 83
- linking, 84
- tool use, 83
Article tool, 83
ATM (Adobe Type Manager)
- Acrobat automatic installation of, 171
- anti-aliasing, 173
- defined, 7
attachments. *See* file annotations
Audio Annotation dialog box, 100
audio annotations, 96, 100
Author field (General Info dialog box), 61
automatic events, 142

B

backgrounds, 125, 184
- check box field, 130
- document, 184
- field color, 125
- graphic, 184
- screen, 136
Batch Operation Progress box (Select a Folder to Optimize dialog box), 161
batch processing, 161
Bookmark Properties dialog box, 74
bookmarks
- creating, 72
- defined, 7, 25, 26
- embedding, within other bookmarks, 75
- icons, 73, 74, 75
- location, changing, 73
- naming, 72
- placement, changing, 75
- properties, changing, 74
- selecting, 73
- viewing, 73
Bookmarks palette pop-up menu, 72–73
- Bookmark Properties command, 74
- Set Bookmark Destination command, 73
borders, 125
Button Options screen (Field Properties dialog box), 140
buttons. *See* radio buttons
byteserving, 162–63
- defined, 160
- prevention, 163
- software versions supporting, 162
- Web server support determination, 162